A *Flight Plan* FOR LIFE

PETER CARROLL

To Tara, Siobhán and Liam

The author will be donating ten percent of his proceeds from this book to:

Cystic Fibrosis is a fatal genetic disease that causes various effects on the body, but mainly affects the digestive system and lungs. At present, there is no cure. However, thanks to the hard work of researchers around the globe, there is new hope within the CF community with the recent development of life-changing drugs. Progress continues towards the goal of one day making CF stand for Cure Found.

To learn more, visit:
WWW.CYSTICFIBROSIS.CA

CONTENTS

"For the great doesn't happen through impulse alone, and is a succession of little things that are brought together."

VINCENT VAN GOGH

CHAPTER ONE

WELCOME ABOARD

"I learned the discipline of flying in order to have the freedom of flight.... Discipline prevents crashes."

CAPTAIN JOHN COOK
British Airways, Concorde Pilot

ABC... Always Be Correcting. This was the advice my flight instructor gave me years ago when I was a student pilot in the Canadian Armed Forces. It was valuable advice for learning how to fly. It turns out that it is also excellent advice for life—the key to finding balance is catching problems when they are small and making the necessary small corrections.

In many ways, life is like flying. Once we take off there are lots of turns, changes of heading, changes of altitude and, for some of us, big changes in attitude as well. Some parts of the trip are nice and smooth but there are also parts where we must buckle our seatbelts as we go through some teeth rattling turbulence. We are all pilots on an incredible journey through life. The key is to manage the challenges on our flight in order to make the most of our time and find joy in the journey.

When my flight instructor said, "In aviation, ABC stands for Always Be Correcting", he was teaching me that smooth flying is the result of keen observation and a sensitivity to changes combined with small corrections in the flight controls. To non-pilots, the instrument panel of an airplane can look like a mess of dials and switches.

Life can often look like a mess too. We get information coming at us from all directions. There is a lot to absorb, but if we pay attention to the right indicators, we often have all the information that is necessary to help us make good decisions.

In flying, a pilot who is paying close attention to the instruments can catch errors early and make the necessary small corrections for a smooth flight. In life, if we catch problems early and make the necessary changes, we can reduce our stress, improve our health, build stronger relationships, have a positive influence on those around us and lead happier lives.

In all aircraft cockpits, you will find basic instruments which give a pilot information on things such as aircraft speed, altitude and heading. It is critical that a pilot continually scans the instruments, particularly when flying in cloud without any outside visual references, in order to keep the aircraft safe and in control. Scanning is a systematic process—if something interrupts the scan and a pilot gets distracted for too long, then bad things can happen. Without visual cues, the inner ear can play tricks on the brain. The pilot might believe that the aircraft is straight and level when in fact it is in a turn, in a descent or even possibly upside down. That is obviously a very dangerous situation.

The lesson for pilots is to continually scan and trust the instruments. Lives depend on it.

In our journey through life, we can easily fool ourselves into thinking that we are flying straight and level when in fact we are not. We can unintentionally put ourselves in difficult situations. We can ignore important information, and even rationalize our choices, until we come face to face with a crisis and often by then it can be too late. Thankfully though, there are "instruments" in our lives that we, like pilots, can systematically scan to catch problems early so that our journey is not only safe but also one filled with happiness and purpose.

Is it reasonable to expect an aircraft to magically stay at a desired air speed, altitude and heading without any need for pilot input? No, of course not. An aircraft's environment is active and constantly changing. There are updrafts and downdrafts. The wind can suddenly change direction. That's all part of flying.

Pilots can't control the wind, but they can control how they react to it.

It would be so much easier if every flight had a tail wind which shortened the trip and every landing was smooth and easy with the wind on the nose. Flying isn't like that, however. Sometimes the only open runway has heavy crosswinds and it's a rodeo ride all the way to the ground. Other times you have to divert around thunderstorms and your arrival time is delayed.

Factors outside of our control are all part of life too.

Shit happens. It just does.

Life is full of challenges which knock us around. The key to a smooth flight, and a well-balanced life, is to keep the scan going, catch problems early and make small corrections.

My flight instructor used to get on my case for sitting on errors. He would say, "If you see an error don't accept it, correct it." You don't magically get back to the desired airspeed, heading and altitude by just looking at and accepting the error. You must respond. You have to do the work. If I didn't catch my errors quickly enough, then I had to speed up my scanning. All the information that I needed was right there in front of me on the instruments. The key to being what is referred to in aviation as "on the numbers" was to keep a good scan going, notice the errors and fix them.

Correcting small errors requires small inputs. Big errors lead to big inputs and that makes for a very bumpy ride. The secret to success was ABC...Always Be Correcting.

Some people might argue that looking for errors in our lives and always trying to correct them puts extra stress on us in what is already a hectic world. However, if we are to find joy in the journey, I believe we must always be looking for ways to achieve balance. Watching out for imbalance does not mean looking at life in a negative way. Despite our best efforts, problems are just a basic part of life.

The goal should not be to eliminate all problems but to be alert to what is going on around us and to catch problems when they are small. Being aware means maximizing the experience and living in the moment.

Working on balance in life is good for our health, our relationships, our finances and our scope of experience. When we focus on achieving balance, we are equipped to take on more and make the most of our limited time here.

It is important to note, though, that leading a well-balanced life does not mean giving all things equal weight. Our interests, skills and experiences are unique to us. How we distribute our time, talents and finances will be unique to us too. What works for one person may not work for another. Our priorities and focus also change as we go through life. New interests, skills and experiences get added to the scales.

Life is an ongoing attempt to find equilibrium—some people even like to say that life is a circus. Well, then make your life a Cirque du Soleil performance with a great story and amazing displays of balance. As the performance unfolds on stage, the act gets more and more complicated and the skills become more and more impressive. Watch the performers closely and you will see they are constantly making small changes in order to keep their balance. They catch errors early, and they correct them. ABC…Always Be Correcting.

In the pages ahead, we will explore some of the "instruments" in our lives that can give us the information we need to find balance with our time, talents and finances. We will explore ways to keep our "scan" going so we can catch problems early and make small corrections to give us a smooth flight. When you make the scan a regular part of your life, you will start to notice things that you may never have noticed before. You will start to appreciate the small things in life because you will be sensitive to how much the small things matter. You will be living in the moment and seeing what I like to call "the extraordinary in the everyday."

The journey ahead requires honesty and hard work. Change always does.

It is a journey of self-forgiveness—we can't change the past, but we can learn from it. If you are way off the airspeed, heading and altitude that you want to be at, you already know it is time to make some changes. They may be big changes at first, but in time you will fine-tune the corrections.

Whatever the weather at your point of departure, one thing you can be sure of is that it's always sunny above the clouds. And with the sun on your face, you can see everything from a new and beautiful perspective.

You are the pilot in control of your life. The controls are in your hands. Make it a great flight!

It starts with the ABCs…Always Be Correcting.

In Flight Check

- Are you ready to come aboard, take to the skies and start your journey?

The freedom of flying has long fascinated man. It captured the imagination of an Italian Renaissance genius named Leonardo da Vinci, who was able to transform his dreams of flight into technical drawings of flying machines. It became an obsession for two bicycle shop owners named Orville and Wilbur Wright who, on December 17, 1903, made the first successful flight in history of a self-propelled heavier-than-air aircraft. Today, it pushes engineers to innovate and design flying machines that go higher, farther and faster than ever before, and it attracts men and women who yearn to break the bonds of earth and experience the joy of flight. Flying has a wonderful history thanks to those who looked to the skies and dreamed. Now it's your turn to take flight and join the ranks of successful aviators.

You are the pilot in control of your own flight. You are in

command. The controls are in your hands. Your destination and the type of flight you have are up to you.

Are you ready?

You can do this!

Before you take to the skies and start applying the ABCs, you need to do something first. You need to do what every pilot does before a flight. You need to check and see if everything is in working order and ready to go. If you are looking to make some changes in your life, then you need to check to see if you are ready for change. You need to do a self-assessment.

Are you serious about making changes? You can't expect anything in your life to change if you don't change yourself.

Flying is not always smooth—it can get bumpy at times and you must be prepared for the turbulence.

Change… just the word can be unsettling and raise our anxiety level. Change is hard, no doubt about it. We resist it. In fact, we are really good at resisting it. However, if we are to unlock our true potential we must grow, and change is integral to growth.

Mistakes will be made along the way. That's OK. That is how we learn. If you aren't making mistakes you probably aren't trying hard enough. Change rarely occurs in a straightforward, linear way. Change is a process and it's often a bumpy process.

Just like the pilot who inspects and assesses the aircraft to make sure everything is solid and will be able to handle being pushed around up in the sky, you need to see if you are prepared to be honest with yourself and if you are truly committed to change.

Several models of change have been developed and researched. I like the following model which breaks the process of change down to five steps:[1]

Awareness

Decision

Knowledge

Ability

Reinforcement

Change always starts with a basic question: why? We need to have an awareness of the need for change in our lives.

Is every part of your life right now exactly how you want it to be?

No one's life is exactly the way they want it to be all of the time. In aviation terms, that would be like walking into the weather office before your flight and the weather report says there are no clouds in the sky, the wind is non-existent, visibility is miles and miles and the seven-day outlook is for more of the same. It is great when it happens, but it is seldom the case. So, if there is a need for change in your life, ask yourself what you would like to change.

Maybe you have been neglecting your health and it is time you started going for regular check-ups and getting serious about exercise. Perhaps you feel overwhelmed by debt and know you need to create a budget and get control of your spending. Or perhaps your job is stressful, and you think you should follow up on the advice of a co-worker who suggested that meditation might help because it did wonders for them. Maybe you want to move to the next level in your career, but you know you must address a skills gap before management will consider you for a promotion. Or perhaps you are in a relationship and you have come to realize that you are not the supportive partner you want to be.

With each of these scenarios, you are asking yourself two very important questions:

Where am I now?

Where do I want to go?

These questions make up your scan. These are the questions you need to continually be asking yourself in order to put ABC into action in your life. Just like a pilot who looks at an altimeter and notices the aircraft is not at the desired altitude, in life we need to tune in to the difference between where we are and where we want to be. We need to see the gap.

The first step on the way to change is to be aware of the need for change. Awareness can come from a variety of sources. A crisis often alerts us to the need for change. When we apply the process of ABC...Always Be Correcting, we hopefully avoid many crises because we are tuned in to catching problems early before they become bigger problems. However, some crises blindside us and completely knock us off our feet, necessitating real and immediate change.

We can also become aware of the need for change as a result

of our communication with others. A family member or a friend might mention they are concerned about the path we are on. Talking with others might show us where we would like to be, and after reflecting on where we are now, we become aware that there is a gap and we have some work to do.

The second step to achieving successful change is making a personal decision to support and participate in the change. We must have the desire to change and make a conscious decision to do so. This step is often the most difficult in the whole process. We cannot be forced to change—we must be willing participants and buy in 100%. Are we willing to shed our old ways and expose our vulnerable self to the world? We might receive the best advice in the world, but it will go nowhere if we don't buy in.

What drives each of us to change is unique and falls along a broad spectrum of motivators. Maybe you want to become more financially secure. Or maybe your doctor told you that your blood pressure is dangerously high, and you need to make some serious changes in your diet and lifestyle. Perhaps you want to learn how to play the violin because it's a dream that you have had since you were little. Whatever your motivation, the important thing is you need to believe that you can achieve the goals you set for yourself.

You need to commit. You need to "burn the boats", an expression that is tied to many ancient myths and military campaigns. Legend has it that when Caesar's army arrived by ship on the coast of England 2000 years ago, the soldiers soon realised they were badly outnumbered by the Celts and fear soon spread through the ranks. When Caesar found his men preparing the ships for a quick retreat instead of preparing for battle, he ordered the boats to be burned. The message to both his army and his enemies was one of absolute commitment to the goal. The only way the soldiers were going to get off the island was to conquer the country—there was no going back. You must do the same if you are to action real change. You must "burn the boats."

Are you all in?

As a sign of commitment, I want you to do something for yourself right now. I want you to write your personal change goal on a piece of paper.

Do it right now.

Place that note in a spot where you will see it every day. You have a much better chance of achieving your goal when you write it down. There is a lot of neuroscience behind why that happens but I am sure we all have examples in our lives where writing down a goal has made it easier for us to achieve it than when it is just floating around in our mind. The note is a commitment to change. It is a way of holding yourself accountable and building resilience.

Remember, you are burning the boats.

This is happening!

The third step to achieving successful change is building knowledge. You need to acquire knowledge on how to get from where you are to where you want to be. Do you need to obtain some training to acquire new skills? Do you need to educate yourself on a subject by reading some books or taking a course?

Maybe the right approach is connecting with an expert who can be your guide and support you through your process of change. You need knowledge on how you are going to get from A to B. In addition, you also need knowledge on how to perform effectively in the future. You need to have the skills and behaviours to support the change and make it stick going forward. Knowledge is a critical step in the change process.

The fourth step to achieving successful change is ability. This is the stage in the process where the change actually occurs. What is the secret path to ability? There isn't one. It is the age-old story of hard work and time. The journey of a thousand miles starts with a single step, followed by another, and another, and another. We set a goal and we work hard to achieve it. This is the stage where you transform knowledge into practical actions to accomplish the change. There will be mistakes made along the way. You have to accept that. It's a learning process in which you try, err, learn, and repeat. You can't acquire the ability to swim by simply reading about the different strokes in a book and never actually practicing in water. You have got to get in the pool and get wet. You have to apply the knowledge.

The final stage to achieving successful change is reinforcement. We must sustain the change. Positive change is about interrupting the habit patterns that no longer serve us and creating new ones. This is easier said than done, though, because we have a natural tendency to revert to what we know. The New York Times best-selling author, Charles Duhigg, says every habit starts with a psychological pattern he calls the "habit loop" which consists of three elements: a cue, a routine, and a reward.[2]

The cue is anything that triggers the habit. It could be a time of day, it could be an emotional state, it could be another person or the environment you are in. The cue tells the brain to go into automatic processing mode. Our brains work on auto mode a lot. The brain knows the satisfaction derived from following the cue. We need to be aware of and track the cues that will trigger the new behaviour in order to reinforce change and create new habit patterns. If you record the details of times you have been successful in actioning a new habit, then you can recreate those situations and more easily reinforce that new habit.

The second element, the routine, is a regularly followed series of actions which in time can lead to the formation of a new habit. If you want to learn how to play the guitar, then the routine could be practicing scales every day. If you want to get in better physical health and achieve your goal of running a marathon, then you need to follow a training schedule which will help you build up to running long distances.

The final element, the reward, is a positive stimulus that makes the brain decide that the previous steps are worth remembering for the future. It is the reason the brain is fine with putting the habit into auto mode. The brain is taking a "been there, done that" approach and knows how the story unfolds. You must reward yourself for sticking with the new habit but be sure to set yourself up for success by setting goals that are achievable.

If we truly buy in 100% and we burn the boats, then we can successfully transition from where we are to where we want to be after going through the five stages of change.

There is no question that enacting change is hard work but there are some highly effective and simple tools that we can use to help us through the process. Many people find journaling is a very effective tool in support of change. It can be very useful for working through thoughts and reinforcing new patterns.

Think of a journal as an ABC process logbook. A journal is a place where you set goals, outline plans, record progress and hold yourself accountable as you reach for new heights. It is a tool you can use for scanning your life to see if you are at the right airspeed, at the correct altitude and heading in the right direction. Writing your thoughts down on paper helps keep your mind organized. It's a way to prioritize problems, fears and concerns. Left to its own devices, the mind wanders and all sorts of thoughts fly through it. Putting pen to paper focuses the mind and helps you live in the moment. The benefit of devoting some time to reflection and recording your thoughts and feelings is that it provides immediate feedback on your day.

Journaling is an excellent practice for alerting you to what needs attention. It is also an incredibly effective approach to stress management. If you are having a bad day, journaling is an excellent way of reducing your stress as it provides an outlet for your emotions. Emotions can be extremely complex, and journaling can help you more fully experience and understand your feelings. Keeping a journal also allows space for positive encouragement and self-talk. You get to record the wins you had over the day and the learning that happened. Journaling is an excellent way to stay motivated.

It is a good idea to read over a journal at regular intervals because as you look back at entries over time you can reflect on your story of transformation. Your journal is a source of positive reinforcement on your journey and a record of your progress. You can review where you have been and compare it to where you are now. You can reflect on life's milestones and appreciate the distance you have travelled along the way.

A journal is also a wonderful outlet for expressing appreciation. Research on gratitude has found that giving thanks and counting blessings can help people sleep better, lower stress and improve interpersonal relationships. When we express our gratitude daily in a journal, we show our appreciation for the little things in life.

When we review the day and ask ourselves, "What happened today? What are my feelings about what happened? What am I thankful for?" we invest important time focusing on the details of life and we become sensitive to the important things, big or small, that make up a day. We begin to see and appreciate the extraordinary in the everyday.

If we don't take the time to promptly reflect, then we can lose the details and often the opportunity for lessons to be learned because we aren't living in the moment.

If you have no idea how to start journaling, here are some tips:

- **Don't edit your thoughts or feelings.** Don't correct your grammar.

- **Don't censor yourself.** Write in bullet points if that's your style.

- **Start small.** You are not writing your autobiography. Jotting down a few ideas and expressing appreciation is a great start.

- **Record your successes, your wins.** Writing down your daily progress helps you appreciate the little victories that add up to big changes over time.

- **Record your daily insights.** Write down your takeaways from the conversations you have, the books you read, the podcasts you listen to, the movies you see etc. Recording deepens the learning.

- **Record your gratitude.** Reflecting on what you are grateful for will heighten the blessings in your life.

- **Find a journaling process that works for you.** Do you have to write every day? No. Some people like to make journaling a daily ritual. Others prefer to set aside a couple of times a week. Maybe 5 minutes every day is your preferred process. Perhaps 30 minutes every few days is your style.

- **Consider adding photographs or quotations that you find inspiring.** Journaling does not have to be restricted to only your own writing. If you are creative, why not also draw in your journal?

Change can be unsettling at first, but it will enable you to become the person you want to be. Change is the precursor to growth.

You don't grow by keeping things the same.

It's OK to be nervous and scared but when you embrace change, life is more exciting. Change leads to new opportunities and new experiences. It is also your ticket out of any situation or any place where you are unhappy or unfulfilled.

The important thing is to never give up.

When you shy away from change, opportunities and experiences pass you by. Remember, you identified areas of your life that you want to change.

Believe in yourself—you are the pilot, the controls are in your hands. If your aircraft is on the wrong heading, then make the necessary inputs to take your life in a whole new direction. ABC…Always Be Correcting.

In the next chapter, we will explore how important it is to invest in yourself. When you invest in yourself, you can earn returns that will last a lifetime.

In Flight Checks

- Is there a need for change in your life? What aspects of your life do you want to change?

- Did you write your personal change goal on a piece of paper and post it where you will see it every day?

- What rewards do you think will work for you in reinforcing change?

- Are you open to journaling? What style of journaling do you think will work best for you and what steps will you take to start?

CHAPTER THREE

WHEELS UP

"Ultimately, there's one investment that supersedes all others: Invest in yourself. Nobody can take away what you've got in yourself, and everybody has potential they haven't used yet."

WARREN BUFFETT

t is absolutely necessary to take care of your mind, body, and soul every day. However, practicing self-care isn't always easy. We seem to be pulled in several different directions on a daily basis. Our lives are busy. With a never-ending list of demands on our time, taking care of ourselves seems to fall way down the agenda and too often slips off entirely.

Has this been happening to you? Is it time you made "me-time" more of a priority?

When I feel self-care is not getting the priority it should in my own life, I like to remind myself of the following little story from the world of aviation. Before take-off on a commercial airplane, the flight crew always ask for your attention while they review the safety procedures of the aircraft. During the presentation, they share a key instruction regarding oxygen masks. They say that in the event of an emergency, put your own mask on first before assisting others. In an emergency scenario on an airplane, if you don't put an oxygen mask on, you have a very good chance of passing out and then you will be the one needing help. The point is that if you don't take care of yourself, you won't be helpful to others for long.

In day to day life, if you focus more on helping others at the expense of taking care of yourself, you will experience stress, fatigue, reduced effectiveness, health issues and burnout.

Self-care is unfortunately associated by many with the idea of selfishness. Wouldn't it be better to see self-care as charging up your energy and allowing you to be highly effective in your interactions with others? It's a lot more comforting to accept a call on your cell phone when your battery is close to 100% than when you are down in the red in the single digits and the first thing you have to say to the caller is, "My battery is really low. I might lose you."

The American Psychological Association (APA) sees physical and mental self-care as such an important issue in patient care that it regards it as an ethical imperative for its members and has included it in the APA Ethical Principles of Psychologists and Code of Conduct.[1] Self-care is critical to staying sharp, motivated and healthy.

How high up are you placing self-care on your daily agenda? I want you to look over this past week and ask yourself how much time was devoted to self and how much to others. What were the things you did that were you-focused? How much time, energy and finances did you set aside for taking care of your mind, body and soul? How much of your time and talents did you share with others?

These are simple questions and ones we seem to hardly ever ask ourselves.

Our lives are busy, and we often don't take the time to reflect. We are racing from one appointment to the next and asking ourselves where the day went. Or, we are so tired from the demands on our time that we fill in the remaining waking hours with mindless entertainment and then sleep for a few short hours before waking up and doing it all over again the next day.

How about scheduling some reflection time?

Reflection time is like the scan I talked about that pilots need to routinely do of their instruments. Get distracted from the scan for too long and you'll find yourself at the wrong speed, heading in the wrong direction at the wrong altitude. For many of us, our scan process is anything but routine. We therefore don't catch the small deviations away from where we want to be. We end up needing to make big corrections when we finally notice our errors, often at a time of crisis, and that makes for a very bumpy flight.

Make a weekly appointment with yourself. Schedule reflection time.

Do it right now.

I'm not kidding.

Stop reading for a minute and set a time every week to reflect on what you did for yourself, how it benefited you, and how you shared your time and talents with others. This time will be completely dedicated to self-reflection. If you commute to work on public transit, that could be your time to reflect. If you are a parent and you have 10 minutes waiting in the car every day when you pick the kids up from school, that could be your time. Choose a time that works for you but make it a habit.

Start your scan. It doesn't have to be long, but it is time set aside to check in with yourself.

Are you where you want to be, or do you need to make changes?

Don't get down on yourself if you've had a bad week and things are well out of balance. Remember, as pilots we don't control the wind, just how we react to it.

Catch those problems early and make the necessary changes to bring balance back. Do the work. ABC… Always Be Correcting!

Focus on the following areas when it comes to investing time in your own well-being. Look at these areas as investment opportunities. You are investing in you. Remember to put your own oxygen mask on first and then you will be well equipped to help others.

EXERCISING

Exercise is one of the most important things you can do for yourself. How important is exercise? The Mayo Clinic lists seven benefits of regular physical activity—exercise controls weight, combats health conditions and diseases, controls mood, boosts energy, promotes better sleep, puts the spark back in your sex life and can be a fun and social activity.[2] For some, exercise can be a hard habit to form. Every January, gyms are loaded with new members who have made New Year's resolutions. However, by the time March rolls around there seems to be no problem getting a machine because for many people the resolutions haven't transitioned to habit. If that has happened to you then maybe you need an exercise buddy or a trainer. Have someone who will hold you accountable. Have someone who expects you to show up. You are much more likely to get out of bed and not cancel that early alarm if you have to explain to your exercise buddy why you didn't hold up your end of the deal.

But exercise is more than just going to the gym, attending a yoga class or buying a pair of running shoes and pounding the pavement in your neighbourhood. Team sports are a great way to exercise too. With team sports, you not only get the physical benefits, but you also get to connect with people and be part of a larger community. Exercise can have both health and social benefits.

You owe it to yourself to devote time to exercise. Your health depends on it. It is important that you consult your doctor and get good medical advice about what exercise is right for you. Set reasonable goals. Choose activities you enjoy. If you enjoy what you are doing, you are much more likely to make it a habit.

If training to complete a triathlon is your thing, that's great, but exercise also includes taking the dog for a walk. My dog, Jasper, reminds me daily how important it is for both of us to get out and exercise. He stares me down with his big brown eyes but if the eyes don't get the message across, he escalates to putting his paw on my lap. Jasper knows we all need a little push every now and then to get going.

The key is to start. *Invest in you.*

WALKING

What do Friedrich Nietzsche, Steve Jobs, Charles Darwin and Ludwig van Beethoven all have in common? They were all big walkers. Nietzsche walked at least 2 hours every day. It was a regular occurrence for residents of Palo Alto to see Jobs walking around the neighbourhood when he was the CEO of Apple. He liked to use the practice of walking to work through problems. Darwin walked a trail near his house every day and called it his "thinking path." Beethoven was obsessed with walking and often walked 3 to 4 hours in the afternoon everyday, rain or shine.

Walking is an excellent way to clear the mind and stir creativity. If you are having trouble focusing on your work or you can't seem to find a novel solution to a difficult problem, go for a walk. It's amazing how a walk can break the logjam and allow creative ideas outside the box to flow.

Walking is also an easy activity that has many positive health benefits. In 2002, the New England Journal of Medicine published a study which showed that 30 minutes of walking briskly, 5 days per week, was enough to lower the risks of cardiovascular disease by up to 30%.[3] Walking increases oxygen flow through the body and it is a good way to boost your energy. It burns calories and is a great low-impact way to stay healthy. Walking may not be a better workout than other physically demanding options, but for some people it may be a better exercise choice.

In our fast-paced modern world, walking is a very underrated form of exercise, transportation, and recreation. Next time you find yourself low on milk, consider walking to the local store rather than grabbing the car keys and driving there. Consider going for a walk on your lunch break and you might be surprised that you have more energy to get you through the afternoon at work. If you find walking a little boring, consider walking with a friend or listening to a podcast or an audio book as you amble along.

Try to make walking a regular activity because it is a very good investment in your personal well-being. *Invest in you.*

READING

The benefits of reading extend far beyond mere entertainment and a way to increase our language skills and knowledge. Reading also improves memory and increases empathy. Research shows that reading makes us feel better and makes us more positive. When we read about a character doing something in a book, we are more likely to actually do that activity in our own life.[4] When we read about heroes, we are inspired. Connecting with characters in a book can also help us in our real-life relationships. David Kidd, lead author of a 2013 Harvard study on reading said, "If we engage with characters who are nuanced, unpredictable, and difficult to understand, then I think we're more likely to approach people in the real world with an interest and humility necessary for dealing with complex individuals."[5]

Would you believe that reading may also lengthen your lifespan? A Yale University study followed more than 3600 individuals over the age of 50 for 12 years. They looked at three different groups: non-readers, people who read less than 3.5 hours per week and people who read more than 3.5 hours per week. The researchers discovered that people who read more than 3.5 hours per week lived on average 23 months longer than non-readers![6]

One of the best things about reading is that the range of styles and genres is so great that there is something for everyone. There's a book for whatever interests you. It is estimated that since Johannes Gutenberg invented the printing press in 1440, over 130 million unique titles have been published. Take a trip to your local library, browse the shelves of your neighbourhood bookstore or search the website of your favourite online book seller and you are bound to find a book that is right up your alley.

Make a plan to sit down with a good book soon because reading is definitely good for you. *Invest in you.*

ENGAGING WITH NATURE

Sir David Attenborough, the British naturalist and media personality best known for writing and presenting nature documentaries, once said, "It seems to me that the natural world is the greatest source of excitement; the greatest source of visual beauty, the greatest source of intellectual interest. It is the greatest source of so much in life that makes life worth living."

Engaging with nature is good for us. Interacting with it, spending time in it, experiencing it, and taking time to appreciate it can make us healthier and happier. We are better for having witnessed a ruby red sunset at the end of a day, listening to the soothing sounds of a babbling brook in the mountains, tasting the sweetness of a freshly picked strawberry growing wild in a field, or feeling the soft lushness of moss carpeting the floor of an old growth forest.

Our affinity to nature is genetic and deep-rooted in evolution. Engaging with nature decreases our stress and makes us feel energized. But it does not only mean hiking mountain meadows—even if the gates to a National Park are not just down the road from where you live, engaging with nature can include taking a walk in a local park. It can mean getting up early and enjoying a cup of coffee listening to the birds from your apartment balcony. Engaging with nature makes us feel like we are a part of something bigger and can put things in perspective. It is also a great way to decompress from the stresses of everyday life. A day at the beach or a weekend breathing in fresh mountain air can provide a much-needed energy boost.

But what can you do if you live in an urban jungle and want to include engaging with nature as part of your daily routine?

A great way to connect deeply with nature no matter where you live is through gardening. Caring for plants can do wonders for your well-being. One of the best aspects of gardening is that you can do it almost anywhere. You can make it fit your available space and budget. The benefits of gardening are not only enjoyed by those with a yard full of flowers and vegetables. You can connect with nature by caring for a small plot in a community allotment, or planting flowers in pots on your apartment balcony or growing some herbs in coffee mugs on your kitchen windowsill. When we roll up our sleeves and get busy digging, planting and weeding, we connect with the rhythm of nature.

A great lesson to be learned through that connection is that we don't control nature. Gardeners all around the world, caring for all types of gardens, face these common truths: they can't control the weather and they can't stop time moving forward. As the great British gardener Monty Don said, "A garden is like a river. It flows, it's always moving, and it's never the same. It never reaches anywhere other than this moment."

Gardening teaches us to appreciate the now and have hope for the future. We can learn a great deal from plants. Plants allow their struggles to make them stronger. A tree exposed to the elements has a stronger root structure than one that has been sheltered from the weather. Plants turn towards the sun. Flowers maximize the opportunity presented to them and bathe in the rays of the sun when it is shining. Plants are adaptable. Gardening makes you acutely aware that time is constantly moving along and to everything there is a season. Plants add value to people's lives. Fruits and vegetables nourish people. Trees offer shade on a hot sunny day and play an essential role in purifying the air we breathe. Flowers add joy and healing through their beauty and medicinal qualities. Nature has a lot to teach us if we take time to connect.

We are a part of nature. We are not separate from it. So, make sure engaging with nature is a part of your routine. Go for a hike, breathe in the salty air of the coast, stroll through a local park on your lunch break from work or plant a seed in a paper cup and watch it grow. You'll be glad you did. *Invest in you.*

PLAYING

You should always find time for the things that make you happy to be alive. In this chapter, we are focused on investing in you, and pursuing interests that make you happy to be alive provides a pretty good return on investment. Do you have a hobby? If not, then now is the time to think about starting one. Everybody should have a hobby. When you have a hobby, you give yourself permission to take some time just for yourself. It is time that is free from any outside expectations or responsibilities. It's "you" time. Hobbies provide the opportunity to pursue something purely for fun. They are activities which bring you joy.

My hobby is photography. When I spend time with my camera, many of my problems and concerns just fade away for a while. Photography reminds me to live in the moment. When I am creating photographs, I must slow down and really look at the world around me. Photography inspires my travel choices, it engages me with nature and it connects me with my community. Pick a hobby that works for you because a hobby is an important part of a well-rounded life.

If you love what you do for a living and consider your work your hobby, I say that's great and I'm happy for you... now go get another hobby. A hobby is not something you do for a paycheque. It is something you do during your leisure time and it takes you out of your everyday experiences. Here are some benefits of having a hobby:

- **Physical:** Hobbies which involve active movement have physiological benefits because they increase both your heart rate and brain function. Other benefits include lower blood pressure, weight loss, building muscle, strengthening bones, and an overall increase in energy.

    Examples: hiking, yoga, any team sport, triathlons

- **Mental and Emotional:** A hobby provides a way to declutter your mind. It can keep you in the moment and take you away from the stresses of the day by focusing you on an activity you enjoy. A hobby can help reduce or eradicate boredom. It gives you something to do when you find yourself with no immediate deadline to fill your time. It also gives you an activity that you can look forward to and get excited about.

    Examples: gardening, painting, cooking, playing an instrument

- **Social and Interpersonal:** A hobby can help your social life and create a bond with others. Hobbies sometimes have clubs or leagues where people with the same interest and specialized knowledge can meet to share experiences.

Examples: dancing, singing in a choir, playing music in a band, playing bridge or chess

- **Creativity:** Some hobbies can inspire you to tap into your creative side. This can be a big benefit if you are unable to express yourself creatively at work. Hobbies can encourage you to stretch the limits of your imagination.

Examples: photography, acting, painting, quilting

Carve out time in your schedule and make it hobby time. Maybe there's something you've always wanted to learn how to do. Maybe you want to take a leap and try something absolutely new. Whatever hobby you choose, just have fun doing it. *Invest in you.*

MEDITATING

The benefits of meditation have been appreciated by many cultures and religions for a very long time. Thanks to the development of brain research in recent years, science is starting to confirm these long-held beliefs in the benefits of meditation with fMRI and EEG data. Meditating is becoming much more of an accepted practice in Western culture. According to a study by the U.S. Centers for Disease Control and Prevention, meditation was identified as the fastest-growing health trend among U.S. adults in 2018.[7] The practice of meditation is known to reduce stress, improve focus, and promote peace of mind.

Bill Gates said in a blog post in 2018 that for years he saw meditation as a "woo-woo thing" and didn't buy into it. He eventually gained a much better appreciation of the benefits and now meditates two or three times a week, for about 10 minutes each time.[8] Hugh Jackman says he was introduced to meditation when he was in drama school and the practice has been an important part of his daily routine for decades. He says the benefit of meditation for him is like pouring a glass of water – at first, it is cloudy but over time that all settles and you see crystal clear through the water.[9] Meditation clears the mind. The cloudiness disappears.

The nature of our minds is to always be working, to always be thinking. If we let our minds wander and run the show it is very easy to get off track. The mind, if not given something to do, will be mischievous.

Can you spare a few 10-minute blocks of time in your week like Bill and Hugh for meditation? You can if you make your well-being a priority. *Invest in you.*

UNPLUGGING

We live in a world of constant contact. We have 24-hour access to news, information and entertainment. We can instantly connect with other people via text, email, phone calls and video chat. Every now and then it is good to unplug. Not just from technology but also from the hustle and bustle of everyday life to physically get away on your own. This is "you" time.

Your options depend a lot on where you live and your comfort level in being truly alone. Going on a solo backcountry camping trip for a few days can be a wonderful experience but it is not everybody's cup of tea.

I was lucky enough to have such an experience when I was training to be a pilot in the Canadian Armed Forces. I was left on my own for a few days in the bush during a survival course that taught me how to live off the land while awaiting rescue. While the experience was challenging at the time, I look on it now as a valuable gift. The opportunity to be completely on your own for days with only your own thoughts and no human contact is a rare experience.

However, unplugging doesn't have to be so drastic. You could grab your car keys and just enjoy a day on the open road. You could pack a lunch and throw a blanket down in a park and enjoy a day alone with a good book. Solitude helps us regulate our emotions and it can have a calming effect that allows us to better engage with others. Time alone can help you develop who you are, your sense of self. It is time with your own thoughts without distractions. In our busy world full of noise, that's a valuable opportunity.

Give it a try. *Invest in you.*

SLEEPING

According to a study by the Centers for Disease Control and Prevention (CDC), more than a third of American adults are not getting enough sleep on a regular basis.[10] The American Academy of Sleep Medicine and the Sleep Research Society recommend that adults aged 18–60 years sleep at least 7 hours each night to promote optimal health and well-being. Not getting enough sleep is bad for you in so many ways. It leads to increased risk of chronic health conditions such as obesity, diabetes, high blood pressure, heart disease, and stroke. For many, stress increases as length and quality of sleep decreases. It's a vicious cycle because increased stress can cause sleep deprivation and the whole situation gets worse. Here are a few tips for getting the quality sleep your body needs:

- **Stick to a sleep schedule:** Go to bed and get up at the same time every day. Try to limit the difference in your sleep schedule on weeknights and weekends to no more than one hour. Being consistent reinforces your body's sleep-wake cycle.

- **Create a restful sleep environment:** Most people get quality sleep in a room that is cool, dark and quiet.

- **Pay attention to what you eat and drink:** Don't go to bed hungry or having eaten a big meal. Also avoid caffeine and nicotine before bed as the effects of stimulants can take hours to wear off.

- **De-stress:** Stress is a stimulus. It activates the fight-or-flight hormones that work against sleep. Give yourself time to wind down before bed and try developing a bedtime ritual that helps you relax.

- **Exercise during the day:** People who exercise regularly sleep better at night and feel less sleepy during the day.

- **Be smart about napping:** A short power nap during the day can be a good thing when your body needs it, but long daytime naps will disrupt your nighttime sleep.

Sleep is a vital component of your overall health and well-being. Take care of yourself and get a good night's sleep. Sweet dreams. *Invest in you.*

TREATING YOURSELF

Think back to when you were a child, and someone gave you some spending money. You would run off to the corner store with a smile on your face in anticipation of your treat—a chocolate bar, a pack of gum or maybe a comic book. You were on cloud nine. Treats are an important part of life. They are little indulgences we give ourselves because... well, no reason needed. You don't need to earn or justify a treat. It is just something nice to get every once in a while. A treat makes you feel good. Isn't that something you should occasionally do for yourself? This is "you" time and you deserve to be happy.

So, pamper yourself with some time at a spa, buy that tub of Chunky Monkey or book that half day off work. Treating yourself is an important part of investing in you. Just remember that by its very definition, a treat is something out of the ordinary. If you are treating yourself all the time, then it's no longer a treat. *Invest in you.*

Investing in yourself may be one of the most profitable investments that you ever make. It gives you a sense of satisfaction and fulfilment. When you invest in yourself, you not only shape the way you interact with the world around you, you also shape the way you see yourself. Invest in you because you're worth it.

In Flight Checks

- What benefits have you experienced from investing in you?

- What new options are you willing to explore?

- How much do you worry about what others think if you invest in you?

CHAPTER FOUR

TRUST YOUR INSTRUMENTS

"What good does it do to be afraid? It doesn't help anything. You better try and figure out what's happening and correct it."

CHUCK YEAGER

rust your instruments! That's the flight school mantra that every student pilot learns. If you fly blind in cloud, without a horizon for reference, you will lose control of the aircraft and that story does not end well.

Trust your instruments!

When you first sit in the cockpit of even the simplest of aircraft, all the instruments in front of you can be very intimidating. The instrument panel is a confusing array of gauges, dials, knobs and digital displays. Everywhere you look there are needles and numbers. To the untrained eye, it's a mess. But to the trained pilot, it is all very valuable information. Everything is there for a reason. Nothing is simply taking up space. The key is to continually scan your instruments, and then use the information to correct any errors and get back on the numbers.

Small errors only need small corrections. However, big errors can lead to a very bumpy flight. ABC… Always Be Correcting.

Dials and gauges are great for pilots but what "instruments" do we have in our own lives that let us know how things are going? What information can we collect to help us catch the small deviations from where we want to be? How do we stay "on the numbers" in our flight through life? Let's explore some "instruments" we can be scanning in life.

MEDICAL HEALTH

When is the last time you had a medical check-up? Are you the type of person that has a complete medical file and always books a yearly medical appointment around your birthday, so you don't forget? Or are you the type that will not see a doctor unless you are rolled out of an ambulance into a hospital, on a gurney by EMTs, because you thought you were as healthy as a horse but you've just suffered a massive heart attack that could have been prevented? Studies show that women are more likely than men to seek out medical care. Ditch the macho attitude men. Get over your fear of body exams. Man up. You should visit your health care provider regularly, even if you feel healthy.

The whole idea of getting yearly medical appointments is for the medical experts to track your medical trends and catch any health problems when they are small. A regular medical exam should be one of the "instruments" you scan in life to see if you are at the proper airspeed, heading in the right direction and at the correct altitude in your flight through life. Just because you feel healthy doesn't mean you are healthy.

According to the National Cancer Institute, approximately 38.4% of men and women in the United States will be diagnosed with cancer at some point during their lifetimes.[1] Early detection gives you the best chance for successful treatment. According to Cancer Research UK, more than 9 in 10 bowel cancer patients will survive the disease for more than 5 years if diagnosed at the earliest stage and many will go into complete remission. More than 90% of women diagnosed with breast cancer at the earliest stage survive their disease for at least 5 years or more compared to around 15% for women diagnosed with the most advanced stage of disease. Close to 90% of women diagnosed with the earliest stage ovarian cancer survive their disease for at least 5 years compared to around 5% for women diagnosed with the most advanced stage of disease. More than 80% of lung cancer patients will survive for at least a year if diagnosed at the earliest stage compared to around 15% for people diagnosed with the most advanced stage of disease.[2]

Avoiding a medical check-up because you fear getting bad news does not make the underlying problem go away. In fact, as the numbers above show it can make a potentially treatable problem much worse. Life is short enough, don't make it shorter by avoiding regular check-ups with your doctor.

You owe it to those you love. You owe it to yourself.

If you have a loved one who does not take regular medical check-ups seriously, then be their co-pilot and point out that they need to make some important corrections. Your efforts may lead to early detection of a medical issue that can be treated.

You should always consult your physician regarding personalized medical advice, but the following tables are handy guides to medical tests and screenings you should consider getting at different stages of your life:[3]

IN YOUR 20S: WOMEN	
Eye Exam	Every 1-2 years: tests for vision, glaucoma and macular degeneration
Hearing Test	Every 10 years: tests ear function
Blood Pressure Screening	Every 2 years: tests risk for heart conditions
Skin Exam	Yearly: tests for signs of skin cancer
Pelvic Exam	Yearly: checks for signs of cancer
Pap Smear	Every 3 years: tests risk of cervical cancer
Breast Exam	Monthly: self-exam Yearly: test for signs of cancer

IN YOUR 20S: MEN	
Eye Exam	Every 1-2 years: tests for vision, glaucoma and macular degeneration
Hearing Test	Every 10 years: tests ear function
Blood Pressure Screening	Every 2 years: tests risk for heart conditions
Skin Exam	Yearly: tests for signs of skin cancer
Testicular Exam	Yearly: tests for signs of testicular cancer

IN YOUR 30S: WOMEN	
Eye Exam	Every 1-2 years: tests for vision, glaucoma and macular degeneration
Blood Pressure Screening	Every 2 years: tests risk for heart conditions
Skin Exam	Yearly: tests for signs of skin cancer
Pelvic Exam	Yearly: checks for signs of cancer
Pap Smear	Every 3 years: tests risk for cervical cancer
Blood Glucose Test	Every 5 years: tests risk for diabetes
Cholesterol Screening	Every 5 years: tests risk for heart disease
Thyroid Stimulating Hormone Test	Every few years: tests for underactive or overactive thyroid
Breast Exam	Monthly self-exam Yearly: test for signs of cancer

IN YOUR 30S: MEN	
Eye Exam	Every 1-2 years: tests for vision, glaucoma and macular degeneration
Blood Pressure Screening	Every 2 years: tests risk for heart conditions
Skin Exam	Yearly: tests for signs of skin cancer
Testicular Exam	Yearly: tests for signs of testicular cancer
Blood Glucose Test	Every 5 years: tests risk for diabetes
Cholesterol Screening	Every 5 years: tests risk for heart disease

IN YOUR 40S: WOMEN	
Eye Exam	Every 1-2 years: tests for vision, glaucoma and macular degeneration
Blood Pressure Screening	Every 2 years: tests risk for heart conditions
Skin Exam	Yearly: tests for signs of skin cancer
Pelvic Exam	Yearly: checks for signs of cancer
Pap Smear	Every 3 years: tests risk for cervical cancer
Blood Glucose Test	Every 5 years: tests risk for diabetes
Cholesterol Screening	Yearly: test for signs of heart disease
Bone Density Testing	Every 3 years: tests for signs of osteoporosis
Mammogram	Yearly: tests for signs of breast cancer
Ovarian Screening	Every 3 years for post-menopausal women: tests for signs of ovarian cancer

IN YOUR 40S: MEN	
Eye Exam	Every 1-2 years: tests for vision, glaucoma and macular degeneration
Blood Pressure Screening	Every 2 years: tests risk for heart conditions
Skin Exam	Yearly: tests for signs of skin cancer
Testicular Exam	Yearly: tests for signs of testicular cancer
Blood Glucose Test	Every 3 years: tests risk for diabetes
Cholesterol Screening	Yearly: tests for signs of heart disease
Prostate Exam	If high risk of prostate cancer

IN YOUR 50S: WOMEN	
Eye Exam	Every 1-2 years: tests for vision, glaucoma and macular degeneration
Blood Pressure	Every 2 years: tests risk for heart conditions
Pelvic Exam	Yearly: checks for signs of cancer
Pap Smear	Every 3 years: tests risk for cervical cancer
Blood Glucose Test	Every 3 years: tests risk for diabetes
Cholesterol	Yearly: tests for signs of heart disease
Bone Density	Every 3 years: tests for osteoporosis
Mammogram	Yearly: tests for signs of breast cancer
Ovarian Screening	Every 3 years: tests for signs of ovarian cancer
Coronary Screening	Yearly: tests for heart disease
Colonoscopy	Every 10 years: tests for colorectal cancer
Fecal Occult Blood Test	Yearly: tests for early signs of colon cancer

IN YOUR 50S: MEN	
Eye Exam	Every 1-2 years: tests for vision, glaucoma and macular degeneration
Blood Pressure	Every 2 years: tests risk for heart conditions
Testicular Exam	Every 3 years: tests for signs of testicular cancer
Blood Glucose Test	Every 3 years: tests risk for diabetes
Cholesterol	Yearly: tests for signs of heart disease
Colonoscopy	Every 3 years: tests for colorectal cancer
Prostate Screening	Every 3 years: tests for prostate cancer

60+ WOMEN	
Eye Exam	Every 1-2 years: tests for vision, glaucoma and macular degeneration
Blood Pressure Screening	Every 2 years: tests risk for heart conditions
Pelvic Exam	Yearly: checks for signs of cancer
Pap Smear	Every 3 years: tests risk for cervical cancer
Blood Glucose Test	Every 3 years: tests risk for diabetes
Cholesterol Screening	Yearly: tests for signs of heart disease
Mammogram	Yearly: tests for signs of breast cancer
Colonoscopy	Every 5 years: tests for precancerous polyps and cancer
Ovarian Screening	Every 3 years: tests for signs of ovarian cancer
Coronary Screening	Yearly: tests for heart disease
Fecal Occult Blood Test	Yearly: tests for early signs of colon cancer
Bone Density Testing	Every 2 to 3 years: tests for signs of osteoporosis
Herpes Booster	Once: prevents shingles
Pneumonia Booster	Once: Protects against pneumonia

60+ MEN	
Eye Exam	Every 1-2 years: tests for vision, glaucoma and macular degeneration
Blood Pressure Screening	Every 2 years: tests risk for heart conditions
Blood Glucose Test	Every 3 years: tests risk for diabetes
Cholesterol Screening	Yearly: tests for signs of heart disease
Colonoscopy	Every 3 years: tests for colorectal cancer or precancerous polyps
Hearing Test	Every 3 years: ear function
Prostate Screening	Every 3 years: tests for prostate cancer
Testicular Exam	Every 3 years: tests for signs of testicular cancer
Bone Density Testing	Every 2 to 3 years: tests for signs of osteoporosis
Herpes Booster	Once: prevents shingles
Pneumonia Booster	Once: protects against pneumonia

NOTE: Beyond these age-specific health screening suggestions, there are also some tests that your doctor might recommend based on your personal health history.

MONITORING YOUR
ENERGY LEVELS

Your energy level is an "instrument" you should monitor. Some days, your energy is completely sapped. Caffeine and grit may have powered you to the finish line, but you have little left in reserve. These are the days when your muscles ache and your eyelids feel like anvils are hanging from them. Your body is exhausted, and you quite happily fall into the arms of Morpheus. These high energy drain days are easy to recognize.

What about the days, though, when you just don't seem to be firing on all cylinders? What about the days when you find it hard to concentrate, when your patience grows short and you are easily frustrated? What about the days when you just can't psych yourself up to do the things that normally bring you so much pleasure? These are the low-grade energy drain days and they can be much harder to recognize.

Here are some ideas for helping to boost your energy level:[4]

- Eating a balanced diet is critical to our energy levels. Keeping your blood sugar balanced is important to keeping your energy constant. Avoid sugar highs because the rapid drops can leave you feeling wiped out. If you are eating well but still feel that your energy levels are low, you might have a slight magnesium deficiency. Always consult your doctor for personalized medical advice.

- When you are low on energy, you might think that

getting some exercise is the last thing you want to do but that is exactly what you should do. A little exercise does wonders for lifting our overall energy levels and mood.

- Take a power nap. A study by NASA in 1995 showed that a 26-minute nap would improve performance by 34% and alertness by 54%.[5] Don't sleep the afternoon away and mess up your night's sleep but a little power nap is good for you.

- Eat three square meals a day. Your car needs gas to go and your body needs food. Don't skip meals or you'll be running on empty.

- Reduce your stress. Anxiety uses up a lot of energy. Low but chronic levels of stress erode your energy levels over time.

- Drink more water.

- Have a power snack. When you reach for a quick treat, try to pick food that combines protein, a little fat and some fiber. The combination works for giving you a quick pick me up while also keeping your energy levels up over time.

- Consult your doctor if low energy is a chronic problem for you. A simple blood test can verify if thyroid dysfunction or anaemia are connected with your low energy level.

It is critical to keep an eye on your energy level as constant low energy might denote a much more serious underlying issue. You should monitor the "needle" on your energy gauge to make sure it doesn't indicate low or, worse yet, empty. By taking steps to correct any issues early, you can ensure you are at full capacity and maximizing your contribution to the world.

LISTENING TO YOUR BODY, LISTENING TO YOURSELF

What does your gut tell you? Trust your gut. I'm sure you've heard this advice throughout your life. However, listening to your body is not as simple as following every thought that pops into your monkey brain. The gut is an "instrument" that needs some calibration if we are to get good information which will help us have a smooth flight. If we listen to every feeling that we have, we could find ourselves off course, unnecessarily overreacting or overcorrecting.

Our bodies can send us signals such as body pain, tiredness, nausea etc. Listening to your body is important. If you find yourself yawning throughout the day, guess what? You are probably tired and you should get more sleep.

Your body is sending you signals. Listen to it.

One of the primary causes of injury is not listening to the body during physical activity. The body sends warning signals and often we don't listen, or we choose to ignore them and push through the pain to our own detriment. When we are mindful of the sensations in our body, we are sensitive to the signals.

Listening to ourselves and deciding whether to follow our intuition is a complicated process. Intuition is a kind of matching game our brain plays based on experience. It is rapid cognition or condensed reasoning that takes advantage, sometimes in error, of the brain's built-in shortcuts. It is an unconscious associative process.[6]

Experience is encoded in the brain as a web of fact, memories and feelings. When we encounter a situation, our brains quickly scan the archives for the best analogue so that we can associate meaning to the situation. The brain is not just accessing knowledge about an experience in our past, but it also incorporates our emotional state of mind at the time and a predisposition to respond in a certain way.

Can this lead to intuition that leads us astray? You bet it can. Our brains can be lazy and only pull certain files from the archive. Our gut reactions can be spoiled by cognitive biases. The problem is that our brain relies on rules of thumb that can often be wildly wrong.

The renowned Nobel Laureate psychologist Daniel Kahneman defines intuition as thinking that you know, without knowing why you do. He suggests that there are three conditions that must be met in order to trust one's intuition:[7]

1. **Regular order:** Kahneman suggests the game of chess is an example where there is regular order. The game has a set of rules, the area of play is set to a standard sized 8 x 8 board and each piece is restricted in how it can move. There is regular order inherent in

the experience gained playing chess. On the other hand, the stock market is an area where intuition should never be trusted. The stock market is not sufficiently regular to support developing any kind of expert intuition.

2. **Lots of practice:** The more time you spend doing something, the better you will get at anticipating outcomes.

3. **Immediate feedback:** Kahneman says, "You have to know almost immediately whether you got it right or got it wrong."

If all three conditions are met, you should trust your intuition. If not, then according to Kahneman, "The mere fact that you have an idea and nothing else comes to mind and you feel a great deal of confidence—absolutely does not guarantee accuracy." So, in summary, should you trust your gut? Is your gut a valid "instrument" in life? Absolutely…under certain conditions.

MANAGING YOUR SCREEN TIME

We live in a hyper-connected world. Screens are everywhere. They are an integral part of how we connect, work and consume our entertainment. However, we should definitely be monitoring and managing our screen time. There is no question that modern smartphones, tablets, computers etc. are incredible tools. Physicist Michio Kaku has said, "Today, your cell phone has more computer power than NASA back in 1969, when it placed two astronauts on the moon."

Like any tool, however, its usefulness or its potential for harm depends on how we use it. When folks waiting at a table in a restaurant all have their heads down and thumbs typing madly on their phones rather than engaging in real conversation with the people right in front of them, then the phone is an obstacle to real human communication and connection. When employees are spending hours each day on social media rather than doing the work they are paid to do, then electronic devices are a distraction that affects focus and productivity. When you spend hours each day glued to your phone and think or say you just don't have the time for any self-care activities, your phone is less of an incredible tool and more of a barrier to you becoming your best self.

A 2018 market research study conducted by OnePoll found that 42% of the time Americans are awake, their eyes are fixated on a television, smartphone, computer, tablet, or other device.[8] It's no surprise that we are staring at screens a lot, but the actual amount of time is pretty alarming. It is almost half the day!

It's a problem, and it's getting worse.

What impact does that amount of screen time have on our health? Staring at screens for extended periods of time can cause Computer Vision Syndrome (CVS). The symptoms of CVS are eyestrain, headaches, blurred vision, dry eyes, neck and shoulder pain. On top of the physical health issues, there is also the negative impact that our screen time can have on our mood.

The trouble with 24/7 access to social media and news outlets is that our boundaries, identities and values can be assaulted whenever we look at our phones. If we do not limit our exposure and we do not control our reactions to what we see online, we can become chronically wound up. We can become irritable and short tempered due to virtual interactions with people we don't even know who push our buttons.

Our relationship with technology is affecting how we develop as individuals and the deeper ways we communicate with others. Dr. Sherry Turkle, professor of the social studies of science and technology at MIT and author of "Reclaiming Conversation", has explored how the constant craving for new information from our phones and computers prevents deep thinking. Time devoted to reflection is being lost. The distractions also prevent deep feeling which lets us connect emotionally with others. According to Dr. Turkle, "If you can't be alone with your own thoughts, you can't really hear what others have to say because you need them to support your fragile sense of self. True empathy requires the capacity for solitude."[9]

The aim should be to balance time alone with our own thoughts with the screen time which is a necessary part of modern life. If you are not already monitoring your screen time, you need to start now. The tools to do this are often found on the devices themselves. Within your phone settings you can see time logs and breakdowns on the activity for each application. Use the information to find a balance because some screen time is simply going to be part of everybody's day in the modern age. We just need to ensure that it does not lead to any health problems and that it doesn't squeeze out time for other important activities in our lives.

LISTENING TO OTHERS

Listening is one of the most important skills we have. We listen to obtain information. We listen to understand. We listen for enjoyment when someone is telling a story or a joke. We listen to learn.

However, listening is not the same as hearing. As Stephen R. Covey once said, "Most people do not listen with the intent to understand; they listen with the intent to reply."

When we listen, we not only open our ears, but we also open our minds to what another person is saying. Good listening connects you with the world around you. Good listening helps you live in the moment. That's why listening is such an important "instrument" in the cockpit of life. When we listen, we can obtain helpful information that might enable us to catch errors when they are small.

Good listening results in stronger relationships. What kind of relationship would you have with someone who talks all the time and doesn't listen to you? You wouldn't have any real relationship at all. If you push people away because you are not a good listener, you could be missing out on some valuable information. Someone with different experiences, different perspectives and different insights can teach us so much if we just listen. It is a gift to have such a strong relationship with someone that they care enough about you to speak the truth to you. These people are the extra eyes in the cockpit of life. They are the contacts in your life that will know when to tell you, and how to tell you, that you are losing altitude.

If we choose to ignore our "instruments" we can find ourselves badly off course in our life, or worse. All the information is there, and it is up to us to pay attention to it. Why make the journey any harder than it has to be?

Trust your instruments!

In Flight Checks

- When is the last time you had a medical check-up? Do you need to schedule an appointment?

- What experiences have you had when you trusted your gut? What have you learned from those experiences?

- In conversation, do you listen waiting for a gap to reply or do you listen with the intent to understand what the other person is saying?

- How are you taking care of yourself in monitoring your health, your screen time and your relationships?

CHAPTER FIVE

CRUISING ALTITUDE

*"Don't judge each day by the harvest
you reap but by the seeds you plant."*

ROBERT LOUIS STEVENSON

S o, what do you do?" It's the standard go-to question people ask each other when they meet for the first time at social events. But work is only a piece of our lives. It is admittedly an important piece considering it is a source of income, an opportunity to socialize and cultivate friendships and a means to develop ourselves. Work can also give us a sense of pride, identity and personal achievement. However, when your job defines you, your world becomes very narrow.

Years ago, I made the decision that "what do you do?" was a question I would never again ask when meeting someone for the first time. Instead, I much prefer more revealing questions—What are you passionate about? What is your favourite travel memory? What inspires you? Thanks to these questions, I have had some fascinating and enlightening conversations getting to know new people.

I do not believe that your job description should be your

self-description. Your job is what you do. It is not entirely who you are. If your job ends up being constantly on your mind, you subtly begin to value people, activities and relationships based solely on how they can help your career.

Your job hopefully gives you great satisfaction and a feeling of accomplishment. However, even in a job you love, you can end up devoting so much time and energy to it that you have nothing left for investing in other areas of your life. That's a problem. Being consumed by work has serious negative effects on your physical and mental health.

A study, conducted by researchers from University College London, compiled data on the relationship between working hours and stroke risk in over 500,000 workers. They found that those who worked more than 55 hours per week were 33% more likely to suffer a stroke, compared with those who worked 35-40 hours per week.[1]

Overwork is a serious concern. It may cost you your life. The Japanese actually have a word to refer to people dying from spending too much time in the office: karoshi, which translates to "death by overwork." And even if overwork doesn't kill you, it can still lead to burnout—a state of emotional, physical, and mental exhaustion caused by excessive and prolonged stress. It occurs when you feel overwhelmed, emotionally drained, and unable to meet constant demands. Burnout on the job involves a sense of reduced accomplishment and loss of personal identity.

The following are some warning signs that you may be too consumed by your work. Think of them as the yellow warning lights on an aircraft's instrument panel which tell the pilot that there is a problem.

- You constantly check emails or messages outside of work.

- You have a minimal number of friends outside of work.

- You don't take vacation days until forced to by management because it's company policy.

- When you do go on vacation, you can't relax because you feel the need to constantly check in with the office.

- You consistently cancel plans with family and friends due to the "demands of the office."

- Working overtime is not an occasional situation for you – it's the standard.

- Your self-image rises and falls with what happens at work.

- Work is all you ever talk about.

- You can't wait for retirement so you can finally start living.

If a couple of these yellow warning lights have lit up for you, then you need to start actioning the ABCs when it comes to your work-life balance. It is time to review your priorities, set new boundaries around your work life and possibly redefine roles and expectations with your employer and at home. If there is no possibility of negotiation, and no hope of change in the long term, then you need to consider seeking a new position which will bring your work life and your personal life into better balance. ABC… Always Be Correcting.

We devote a lot of time and energy to work so it is important that we closely monitor our work situation throughout our lives. It is important to keep your work scan going to ensure you are at the desired airspeed, heading in the right direction, and at the correct altitude when it comes to your work life.

Work is different things to different people. For some, it's just a job and a paycheque. Work pays bills and puts food on the table. For others, work is a method of self-expression. They feel an authentic connection between the work they do and a broader life purpose beyond their own self-interest.

All work is honourable. Some people work in large companies in huge office towers and others are self-employed and work from home. Some work under short term contract situations and others are full-time employees. Some are government workers and others enjoy roles in the private sector. Everybody's situation is different. Maybe you are perfectly content in your present job. The pay meets your financial needs and you feel fulfilled in what you do. Perhaps your work is fairly mundane, but you are not so concerned about self-expression at work because you have found plenty of ways to fulfil those needs outside of your employment. Possibly you see your job as a temporary situation and a necessary steppingstone to future opportunities. Or maybe you are working your dream job and you could not imagine working with a better group of people. If your employment works for you, great!

What can or should you do though when you feel that work simply isn't working for you?

Moving to a new position or moving jobs is a big decision. It should not be made without significant discussion, reflection and a plan.

The following are some signs you should be aware of which indicate it might be time for you to move on and find a better work fit:

- You believe that your work-related stress is affecting your physical and mental health.

- There is no improved future for you at the company: You feel powerless over your career and you see no room for development or advancement.

- You and your work are being undervalued.

- Your work performance is suffering: This might be because you are bored in your work duties or because your efforts go unrecognized, unrewarded, blocked or ignored.

- You are experiencing verbal abuse, sexual harassment, or are being discriminated against on the basis of your race, sex, religion, disability or other protected class.

- You feel miserable in your position and you dread going into work.

Sometimes, after working within an organization for some time, you might find that you just do not fit in with the corporate culture. A corporate culture is the shared values, attitudes, standards, and beliefs of the organization. It is rooted in an organization's goals and structure. A culture is an organization's personality, and just like relationships outside of work, sometimes personalities clash. As you progress through different stages in your career, specific cultures can become more or less appealing based on your personal goals. Culture manifests itself in an organization's approaches to labour, customers, investors, and the greater community.

There are 4 basic culture types:[2]

- **Clan:** The atmosphere is friendly and collaborative. The organization feels like a large family where people have a lot in common.

- **Adhocracy:** Employees are encouraged to take risks and aggressively pursue new ideas. Organizations with adhocracy culture live by the "move fast and break things" philosophy.

- **Market:** The goal is to get down to business, get work done, and achieve results. Leaders are tough and demanding and the work environment is often competitive. The purpose of being at work is to make as much profit and capture as much market share as possible.

- **Hierarchy:** Process and procedure is everything.

Leaders are in place to ensure that their teams run like well-oiled machines following tried and true business practices.

An organization's culture is what it is. It will change only slowly, and it will not change to suit you. Organizational cultures can indeed change with strong leadership but changing the culture of a company is like turning a giant ship. It takes lots of effort, and time. If you have made honest efforts to fit in with the organizational culture but are still impeded in your ability to succeed in the job, then it's probably best for you to move on.

No work situation is without its problems. Any decision to move on should not be arrived at without applying the ABCs within the job first. Talking through problems, aspirations and goals with a boss, addressing concerns directly with co-workers and talking to Human Resources, when applicable, are options that should be explored to try and resolve issues.

You should also look into the possibility of connecting with others in a mentor network. You might find such networks within the company you work for or you could connect with others in your field through a professional organization. A mentor network can be a wonderful support as you go through difficult periods at work. It is comforting and empowering to connect with others who have, through experience, an appreciation and understanding of what you are going through. If in the end there is no hope of a better work environment, and work is just not the right fit, then it is time to move on.

If you get to this stage, consider seeking out the help of a professional career advisor. Moving on to a new job is a big step and you do not want to replace the poor fit of one role or work environment with another. A career coach can give you valuable insight into your career development and trajectory. With the help of a career coach, you can assess your skills and identify gaps which might hamper you achieving your career goals. A career advisor can offer you advice on the style of resume and cover letter that will have an impact with modern recruiters and also help you prepare for the interview process so you present yourself in the best possible way to potential employers.

How can you as an individual employee apply the Always Be Correcting approach in the workplace? With respect to your present job, are there any skills you would like to improve in order to do your job more effectively? What are the skills you would need to add to your present skill set in order to be considered for promotion? What about job opportunities down the road with other employers? Do you have the skills recruiters are looking for when they hire for your dream job?

Successful people make themselves aware of what they will need to know and do to succeed in the next job. Look into taking advantage of training opportunities within your company to add to your skill set. The logic behind the saying "dress for the job you want not the job you have" also applies to skills. If you are unsure of what career options are available to you with the skills you have, or will have with a little training, then you should consider a skills assessment. There are tests available which can give you guidance on the types of jobs you should consider. You always want to be marketable to an employer so it's important to stay up to date with the latest knowledge in your area and to add to your skill set as you progress in your career.

It is also good to be prepared in case a great opportunity presents itself or you unfortunately find yourself without a job, due to circumstances outside of your control. Part of being prepared is having your resume up to date and ready to go. You do not want to be caught flat-footed when your dream job opens up or you get called into the boss' office to receive the news that you have been laid off.

Always be prepared.

Every time you add a significant new skill or change your job title, you should update your resume. Keep a PDF copy on your phone so if you meet someone at a social event you have the option of immediately forwarding a copy. If you have an updated version ready to go and you get the unfortunate news that you have been laid off, then you can put your energy into searching for a new job rather than frantically scrambling to update a resume that might be a decade out of date. You should also keep your social media profiles up to date. Smart employers passively recruit all the time by searching sites such as LinkedIn for talent.

Always represent yourself in the best possible way. Always be ready for opportunities.

ABC… Always Be Correcting.

We spend so much time at work that it is important to focus on the ripple effect it has on other aspects of our lives. We need to keep our work lives in perspective and to always strive for balance. You may love your job but nobody on their death bed said they wish they had spent more time at work. And if work isn't working for you, then do everything you can to take advantage of better opportunities.

In Flight Checks

- What changes, if any, do you need to make in order to have a better work-life balance?

- Do you see a future for advancement with your present employer? If not, are you OK with that or do you need to create an action plan?

- What are the skills needed for your dream job? Do you already possess the skills an employer would be looking for or do you have a skill gap you need to address?

CHAPTER SIX

FUEL ONBOARD

*"The price of anything is the
amount of life you exchange for it."*

HENRY DAVID THOREAU

You can fool your friends, you can fool your family and you can even sometimes fool yourself about your financial situation, but you can't fool your banker. Your banker knows your financial truth and you should too. When you apply for a loan, your banker looks at your financial instrument panel and knows your numbers. The bank wants to limit its risk when lending money, so it needs to know if you are at the proper airspeed, heading in the right direction and at the correct altitude, financially speaking. The bank doesn't have access to any more information than you can find out yourself, but the majority of people rarely take the time to really look at their overall economic situation until it's time to apply for a loan.

Your banker is not seduced into thinking you are low risk for a loan and financially secure by the fancy car your drive or the expensive beach vacation you just came back from. Other people in your life might be impressed, but not your banker. Your banker is impressed by your credit score and your net worth:

your assets minus your liabilities. Your financial truth is all there on your personal balance sheet.

Money is a taboo subject for many people. It is considered gauche to discuss money if you are the one with more and money is unfortunately the way much of the world keeps score in the game of life. Many people feel embarrassed if they have less money than others. The result is that money is seldom discussed honestly. This often leads people to lie to others, and worst of all, to lie to themselves.

Remember, if a pilot does not keep a regular scan going on the instruments, gets distracted for too long and then makes incorrect inputs, the aircraft could actually be upside down and diving at the ground. That can also easily happen when it comes to money.

Bad money decisions, compounded over time, can lead to flying your finances into the ground.

What you choose to spend your hard-earned money on is up to you. That's money you have. The problem is that many people are borrowing and spending other people's money on a lifestyle they can't afford. They are digging themselves a massive hole and burying themselves alive. It's time to take away the shovel.

If you are lying to yourself about money, it is time to stop because money problems don't magically go away. They get worse.

According to the American Psychological Association (APA), concern about money is the top cause of stress in the United States. In a 2015 survey, the APA reported that 72% of Americans stressed about money at least some of the time during the previous month.[1] Financial anxiety can lead to health problems such as high blood pressure, headaches, chest pain, insomnia and depression. It's time to get real about money.

Do you have a solid idea right now where you stand financially?

Do you have a plan when it comes to your money?

Are you in a good place financially or is it time to make some corrections?

The world of money is one often loaded with numbers, tables and graphs. Economists love getting lost in the weeds of economic data. To most of us, however, the data is all just white noise and we simply want answers to questions such as: Will I qualify for a mortgage and if so, how much? How do I create some savings? Will I be able to finance a vehicle? What will my retirement years look like financially? There are some basic financial indicators that the average person can use to assess their financial health.

Let's explore some of the financial instruments that bankers look at to determine the airspeed, heading and altitude you are flying at financially speaking. What are the markers that tell us if we are on the numbers or if a correction is in order? Remember… ABC… Always Be Correcting.

NET WORTH

The first place to start is your net worth. What does your overall financial picture look like? If you walked into a bank looking for a loan, your net worth is where a banker would start in order to get a picture of where you stand financially. Your net worth is the difference between your assets and your liabilities – simply put, it's what you own minus what you owe.

NET WORTH = TOTAL ASSETS – TOTAL LIABILITIES

Let's start with the assets:

1. The first thing to calculate is the amount of liquid assets you have. Liquid assets are those you could easily access if you needed cash right away. These are things like your chequing and savings accounts and any money you have stuffed under the mattress (not a recommended approach to savings by the way).

2. Next, you want to calculate your investment assets. Do you have any stocks, bonds, GICs etc? Add up all your investments both inside and outside of a registered retirement account.

3. Lastly, you want to add up all your personal assets. These are things that have value but are difficult to turn into cash quickly, such as: your principal residence, other property you own, valuable items (jewellery, electronics, furniture and appliances, art and other items that have a high resale value), vehicle(s) etc. It is important that you only consider the current value of these items. Do not use what you paid for the items or what you think they might be worth in the future. Only consider the fair market value of the items if you tried to turn them into cash now.

You are looking to calculate your present net worth not some possible best-case scenario. It is a good idea to look at your net worth every so often because the values of some of the items you are adding up are affected by market fluctuations and possible depreciation over time. Your local real estate market might have taken off or dried up since you last calculated your net worth. For most people, their principal residence carries great weight in their net worth calculation. Any stocks you own might be doing very well because the market is bullish or maybe your stock portfolio tanked because of an economic recession.

In summary, for assets we have:

TOTAL ASSETS = LIQUID ASSETS + INVESTMENT ASSETS + PERSONAL ASSETS

Now you need to calculate what you owe. You need to add up all your liabilities:

1. For most people, the biggest liability on their balance sheet is the mortgage on their home. You need to find out the current balance owing on your mortgage. A good financial argument can sometimes be made for renting and not purchasing a home depending on your stage in life, local house prices, the local rental market and what you do with the money you save in rent compared to using it to pay a mortgage. For the

purpose of net worth through we are only looking at the liability of any current mortgage balance.

2. Next you need to add up all the balances owing on any credit cards.

3. Finally, you need to add up all the current balances owing on all other loans: auto loans, student loans, lines of credit etc.

In summary, for liabilities we have:

**TOTAL LIABILITIES = MORTGAGE +
CREDIT CARDS + OTHER LOANS**

Now that we have values for Total Assets and Total Liabilities, we can calculate Net Worth:

NET WORTH = TOTAL ASSETS – TOTAL LIABILITIES

Now that you have a net worth number you have a big picture view of where you are financially. According to the 2016 Federal Reserve Survey of Consumer Finances, a household in the U.S. had an average net worth of $692,100.[2] That number may be shocking and lead you to think you are in trouble but don't fret yet because that is the mean, or average, calculation and it is skewed by the nation's super rich. The median calculation is a better guide as to where you stand financially relative to friends and neighbours. The median is the middle point in the data where half the households have more, and half have less. The median net worth of the average U.S. household is

$97,300. Be careful about feeling elated if your net worth is higher than this because households living "below the poverty line" skew this calculation also. Our net worth changes as we move through different stages in life. The survey broke down the median and average net worth by age:

AGE	MEDIAN NET WORTH	AVERAGE NET WORTH
Under 35	$11,100	$76,200
35-44	$59,800	$288,700
45-54	$124,200	$727,500
55-64	$187,300	$1,167,400
65-74	$224,100	$1,066,000
75+	$264,800	$1,067,000

Calculating your net worth is something you should do every few years. There are several apps for your phone or tablet which make the process of calculating net worth very easy. Hopefully, your net worth grows as you get settled in your career and make various investments that increase in value over time. Tracking your net worth is part of your scan that you can do to monitor if your flight, financially speaking, is on the numbers of if you need to make some corrections.

MANAGING DEBT

Debt help organizations are telling us that North Americans are drowning in debt. Now, not all debt is bad. Debt is not the monster under the bed if you approach it in a financially reasonable and educated way. Debt is, in essence, a financial instrument that allows you to receive and use money now and give it back in the future with a borrowing cost added into the repayment. Borrowing money to get an education that will get you started in a career you love with a great salary or taking out a mortgage to purchase a home you can afford so that you are paying down your own mortgage instead of paying off someone else's can be good decisions.

Debt is often simply referred to as either good or bad. Good debt increases your net worth or has future value. Historically, mortgage debt is the classic example of good debt. Bad debt is money you borrow to spend on things that may provide gratification, but which do not increase in value over time and in fact decrease net worth. Taking out a high interest loan to pay for a holiday that then takes you years and years to pay off would be an example of bad debt. Putting aside a little bit of every paycheque and saving it in a travel fund for your well-earned vacation is a better plan.

In early 2020, the Federal Reserve Bank of New York indicated that American household debt levels were at a record level of $14.15 trillion.[3] The total debt owed by an average U.S. household is closing in on $139,000. When it comes to debt, a financial instrument that bankers use is your Debt-to-Income (DTI) ratio. DTI measures your ability to manage monthly payments to repay the money you borrow. Lenders always want to minimize their risk of a loan going bad, so DTI is an indicator of your ability to manage the monthly payments to repay the money you plan to borrow. DTI is calculated by adding up all your monthly debt payments and dividing by your gross monthly income which is your income before taxes. Government and individual banking rules are different depending on where you live but generally lenders like to see the DTI less than 42%. A maximum DTI of 35% is deemed acceptable when taking only housing costs into consideration. Here's a general overview of the number ranges:[4]

> Good: 36 percent or less
> Manageable: 37 percent to 42 percent
> Cause for concern: 43 percent to 49 percent
> Dangerous: 50 percent or more

Note: These general parameters will also be modified by lenders based on overall economic conditions such as recessions, corporate bankruptcy rates, the inflation rate, personal age group, etc.

If you don't know your DTI ratio you should. DTI is like one of those cockpit instruments you should be scanning when it comes to your financial health. The following is a sample calculation:

DEBT TO INCOME (DTI) RATIO CASE STUDY

Monthly debt payments: Mortgage $1200
Car loan $400
Other debts $800

Gross monthly income: $6000

$$DTI = (1200 + 400 + 800) / 6000$$
$$= 0.40$$

A DTI ratio of 0.40 is manageable, but if more debt is taken on without an increase in income it could be cause for concern. If your DTI is high, what corrections can you make to improve it? Remember ABC… Always Be Correcting. You have two basic options: 1. Lower your total monthly debt payments and/or 2. Increase your gross monthly income. Calculating the DTI ratio can be a very good wakeup call for many people about where they stand financially. Your DTI ratio is a great financial instrument to monitor. It should be part of your financial scan to determine if changes need to be made.

Remember, you are flying the plane… don't let the plane fly you!

CREDIT SCORE

Another cockpit instrument you should be monitoring when it comes to your financial health is your credit score. A credit score is a three-digit number, typically between 300 and 850, which is designed to represent your credit risk, or the likelihood you will pay your bills on time. In general, a higher credit score represents a higher likelihood of responsible financial habits. Credit scores are one of many factors used by lenders when determining your likelihood of paying back a loan. The three major credit bureaus in North America are Equifax, Experian, and TransUnion. The following factors are considered by the bureaus when they calculate your credit score:

- The number of accounts you have

- The types of accounts you have

- Your used credit vs. your available credit

- The length of your credit history

- Your payment history

Each credit bureau has its own algorithm it uses to weigh each of these factors and not all lenders report to all three credit bureaus so you might see some different results in the final number provided by each bureau. How do you find out your credit score? There are several ways you can go about it. One way is to purchase your credit score directly from one of the three major credit bureaus identified above or other provider such as FICO. Another is to check your credit card or loan statements. Many credit card companies, banks and loan providers have started providing credit scores to their customers. It may be provided either on the loan statement or on the online account. Another way to get your credit score is by signing up for one of any number of free credit services. As with all "free" services, make sure to read the small print first.

So you have your credit score, what does that three-digit number say about you? Credit scoring models vary and lenders have their own score thresholds for lending to customers but, in general, credit scores from 660 to 724 are considered good; 725 to 759 are considered very good; and 760 and up are considered excellent.

CREDIT REPORT

Another important financial instrument you should be monitoring in association with your credit score is your credit report. The credit score is a three-digit number and the report reflects a summary of your credit history as reported to credit bureaus by lenders and creditors. There are four general sections to a credit report:

- **Identifying information:** This section includes personal information, such as your name, address, Social Security Number, and date of birth.

- **Credit accounts:** This section lists all your accounts by type (for example, credit card, mortgage, student loan, or auto loan), the date you opened the account, your credit limit or loan amount, the account balance, and your payment history.

- **Inquiry information:** This section lists all inquiries made by companies requesting information from your credit report.

- **Bankruptcies and collection information:** This section lists bankruptcies and past-due accounts that have been turned over to a collection agency.

You are entitled to a free credit report every 12 months from each of the three major credit bureaus. All the information on how to order your free credit report can be found on the individual bureau websites. In the United States, you can also request your annual report through the website www.AnnualCreditReport.com.

Why should you monitor your credit score and credit report? One reason is that the information provided by both gives you a picture of where you are financially and the perspective that potential lenders have of you, if you apply for a loan. It is important to be honest with yourself where you are financially. Are you on the numbers or do you need to make some corrections? ABC… Always Be Correcting.

Another reason to monitor your credit score is that you want to make sure there are no errors on your report. According to a study by the Federal Trade Commission, about one in four people identified potential errors that might affect their credit on one of their credit reports.[5] Errors do happen. You don't need an error on your report dragging down your credit score resulting in you being denied a loan. If you find an error in your report, you can find information on how to file a dispute on the individual credit bureau websites as well as www. annualcreditreport.com.

Reviewing your credit report regularly will potentially also alert you early to identity theft and credit card fraud. You want to make sure all the listed accounts are yours and any that you have closed out are not showing up as still active.

BUDGETING

We have had a good look at the big picture financial instruments you should be monitoring. Your net worth, credit score and credit report will tell you, from a financial perspective, if you are at the proper airspeed, heading in the right direction and at the correct altitude. What about more day to day monitoring? This is where the small input changes come in which help you have a smooth flight. Poor financial decisions made repeatedly day after day add up over time and require big corrections.

The best way to monitor your spending over the short term and plan for the long term is to have a budget. A 2013 Gallup Poll found that only one in three Americans prepare a detailed household budget.[6] Remember what happens to the plane when a pilot is not monitoring the instruments and gets distracted? It does not end well. Having a budget helps to keep your spending in check and makes sure your savings are on track for the future.

The following are some basic steps to creating and living within a monthly budget:

Review your financial paperwork: You are going to need information found on your pay stubs, bank statements, credit card bills, loan statements, utility bills, recent receipts etc

Calculate your income: If you get a regular paycheque then the amount your employer deposits in your bank account every month is the number to use though remember that gross income before tax is used in the DTI calculation. However, if you have set up automatic contributions to a retirement fund with your employer then add this amount back into your take home pay. You will put the automatic retirement fund contribution amount under savings in your budget, so you get a true picture of your efforts in saving for the future. Remember to include all sources of income such as child support, social security or any income from a side-hustle. If you have variable income, then it is suggested that you use the lowest-earning month over the past year as your monthly baseline income.

Create a list of monthly expenses: Use your bank statements, receipts, and credit card statements from the last three months to identify all your spending. Some suggested categories include: mortgage payments or rent, car payments, property taxes, insurance, groceries, utilities, internet, cell phone, entertainment, personal care, eating out, childcare, clothing, transportation costs (bus pass, fuel, repairs and maintenance, registration fees etc.), travel, student loans, savings, emergency fund, education, medical expenses, household maintenance and improvements, charitable contributions, etc. (Note: For some people, expenditure tracking can be a useful approach at a higher level than budgeting and only expanded to a more expenditure-detail level when an over-spending problem is identified.)

Determine fixed and variable expenses and assign values to categories: Fixed expenses will be the same month to month such as your mortgage or rent, insurance, car payments etc. Variable expenses will change month to month and will include categories where you have more discretion over the spending such as eating out and entertainment. Now you need to assign values to the various categories. Start with the fixed expenses and then assign values to the variable expenses.

Determine your delta: The delta is the difference between your income and your expenses. If your income is higher than your expenses, then you are in a good situation. You can take the difference and put it towards savings, paying off debt, investing or celebrating. If your income is lower than your expenses, then you are overspending, and you need to make some changes. The first place to look at making changes is your variable expenses. Where can you trim? Eating out? Entertainment? Vacation? New vehicle? Trimming expenses can be hard but a budget is a financial instrument that tells you the truth about your financial situation. Creating and following a budget will tell you if you are flying at the proper airspeed, heading in the right direction and at the correct altitude when it comes to your money.

Monitor: So, you've done the work and budgeted an amount for each category. Now the challenge is to stick to it. There are a few ways you can do this, and you need to pick the one that works for you.

The "envelope budgeting system" is an old school one where in a cash-based system you get a bunch of envelopes and you write your budget category titles on separate envelopes. Then you fill each envelope with the amount of cash you have budgeted for that category for the month. The idea is you can only spend the money in the envelope on your purchases that fall into that category. Our society has moved away from cash payment and if you like to pay with card or your phone then this system may not be satisfactory for you. There is also the personal safety aspect to consider when you are walking around with cash or known to hold cash in your house. The modern practicality of the envelope budgeting system may be in question but as a concept it works because it is a very real reminder of money already spent and how much remains. When it's gone, it's gone.

A new school way of monitoring your budget and your spending is to use an app on your phone. Many banks have great apps they make available to customers which help keep track of spending. There are also apps you can buy on the App Store or Google Play which are very helpful in tracking your spending and encourage keeping you on budget. Some apps allow you to snap a photo of your receipts and enter details of the items that were bought. The app will log the receipt and enter the amounts spent in the applicable categories. You can often set up alerts within the apps to notify you when you have reached different levels of your spending for the month. It is helpful to get an alert that says you've spent 75% of your budgeted amount for eating out when there are still three weeks left in the month. The app keeps you up to date on where you stand and with real time information on your phone you can adjust your spending, stay on budget and not overspend.

Revisit: Every couple of months or when a significant financial event happens, it is a good idea to revisit your budget and update as required. If you pay off a loan, you will need to update the budget and allocate the money that used to go towards that loan payment to a different category. Could you add it to savings? Could you increase payments on another loan and pay off that debt quicker? Could you now afford to purchase some postponed item because you are operating under good financial control?

Saving and spending is a balancing act. It's more fun to spend but the secret to financial stability is to live within your means. We often know what we should do when it comes to money, but it is too easy to make poor choices. Pre-approved credit card applications show up in the mail when we are having money problems and simply by completing a form, we have access to high interest credit. The car salesman in the showroom hears we want the entry level model but when it comes to the test drive all they have available is the top of the line model and we fall in love with the car we can't really afford.

When my children started working part-time jobs and making some spending money, I gave them a piece of advice that was inspired by the quotation at the beginning of this chapter by Henry David Thoreau—"The price of anything is the amount of life you exchange for it." I told them when you are considering spending your hard-earned money on something, stop and consider if the item is worth the time you put into earning the money you are about to spend. If you are looking at a new pair of shoes that cost $150 and you make $15 per hour after taxes, are the shoes worth 10 work hours to you? What if you use a credit card to buy the shoes? As long as you use credit responsibly, there are many advantages to using it as a purchasing tool. However, if you don't pay off the balance when your credit card bill eventually comes in, then interest gets added month after month and those shoes end up costing you a lot more than 10 work hours.

SAVING

We have looked at money from a spending perspective, and how to live within your means and stick to a budget. Now let's look at the other side of the coin—saving. For many, the hardest part about saving is simply getting started.

The answer is to "pay yourself first."

This means putting money right from your paycheque into your savings or investment accounts before you spend it on anything else. Think of the "pay yourself first" savings as a bill that needs to be paid. When you look at it like that, saving can change from a desire to a necessity. When saving becomes a habit and over time you see the impact on your net worth, you come to appreciate the connection between money, time and compound interest. If you can get in the habit of saving a little bit of every paycheque at a young age, it can lead to great things.

What kind of great things? Well, if at the age of 20 you started with a deposit of $1000 and every two weeks you took $100 from your paycheque and added it to the deposit and you were able to get an annual rate of return of 5% you would have a balance of over $434,000 by the time you were 65. If you were able to get an annual rate of return of 8% you would have over $1,000,000! That's the power of compound interest, continual saving and time. Let's take a look at how powerful the continual saving part is to the final balance. Let's say your friend, who was also

20, liked the idea of putting $1000 into savings but never added $100 every two weeks like you did, he would have a balance of just under $32000 if he was also able to get an annual rate of return like you of 8%. You end up with over $1 million and he ends up with under $32k. Over the 45 years your total deposits equalled $118,000 but your growth was $956,000! That's the power of compound interest, consistent saving and time. Now, maybe you don't have $1000 to start and maybe after making up your budget you truly can't afford $100 every two weeks. Just start wherever your starting point is and add what you can. The key is to start. Do more when you can do more. Just get in the habit of saving and making your money work for you.

Contrary to popular belief, money won't make you happier. Wealth is an amplifier and a force multiplier. It's not the source of happiness. I like to say money makes who you are bigger. If you are a jackass, then lots of money will make you a bigger jackass. If you are a good person, then lots of money helps you have even more of a positive impact on the world.

Money is an important tool of exchange in life, so it is important to not waste it and with good financial knowledge make the most of what you have. The title of this chapter is "Fuel Onboard" and it was chosen for the section on money for a reason. Pilots have a saying – the three most useless things in aviation are: fuel left in the fuel truck, runway behind you and sky above you. Money is your fuel onboard. It helps you to get where you want to go. There's no point setting off on a long flight and looking at the fuel gauge still a long way from your destination wishing you had put more fuel in the tanks.

In Flight Checks

- Do you have a financial plan, or do you feel things are out of control when it comes to your money?

- How would you describe your relationship to money?

- What grade would you give yourself when it comes to your general financial knowledge? How do you plan to increase your financial knowledge and discipline?

CHAPTER SEVEN

AIR TRAFFIC CONTROL

"I get by with a little help from my friends"

JOHN LENNON AND PAUL MCCARTNEY

On my first solo flight in jet training, I had to radio the tower and declare an emergency because a warning light lit up on the aircraft's instrument panel. Air traffic control (ATC) notified Emergency Response Services at the airport while I focused on flying the aircraft and bringing it in for a safe landing. As I landed the jet, the fire and medical trucks were racing down the runway behind me. In the end, maintenance found that the warning light was due to a faulty sensor but it sure was nice to know that I was part of a team and that everyone was quick to respond and ready to help me. In life, like in flying, we can't do it all on our own.

We all need some help every now and again.

Asking for help when you need it is one of the kindest things you can ever do for yourself. Unfortunately, asking for help is seen by many as a sign of weakness. In fact, true strength is having the courage to ask for help. It's not easy, but it is very important.

Often, we self-sabotage our own efforts and make it much harder to do the things we want to do. We could have a better experience and more consistent results if we just got out of our own way.

Perfectionism and a lack of confidence are huge barriers to asking for help. Culturally, perfectionism is even seen in some circles as a positive trait. It's even a stock answer to the terrible interview question—"What's your greatest weakness?." Perfectionism has been defined as the setting of unrealistically demanding goals accompanied by a disposition to regard failure to achieve them as unacceptable and a sign of personal worthlessness[1]. Perfectionism is driven primarily by internal pressures such as the desire to avoid failure or harsh judgment.

However, perfectionism is a huge burden and it can be exhausting. Perfectionists have an all-or-nothing approach, and while it seems paradoxical, they can be prone to procrastination due to fear of "failure." They are hindered by thinking that if something can't be perfect then why start at all. They take constructive criticism defensively so asking for help is a problem. On the other hand, those who naturally seek out help when they need it often see criticism as valuable information which will improve their future performance. Perfectionists are so focused on getting to the mountain top that they don't appreciate their achievements and the accompanying majestic views at different stages on the climb.

If you are highly self-critical, think in absolutes, are stressed all the time and always notice what everyone else is doing wrong, take heart. Reigning in perfectionist tendencies is totally achievable. Here are some ideas to help you start:

- **Give up control:** Purposely choose to cede some tasks to other people. When you see others succeed using an approach that you wouldn't naturally choose, you will grow to appreciate that there are many pathways to success. There is seldom one and only way. You will begin to enjoy process as well as outcome.

- **Be careful when comparing yourself to others:** Comparison can be unfair because we are often making comparisons on little or no evidence. Social comparison is inevitable. We are hardwired for it. Just remember that you might not have the full picture.

- **Focus on the positive:** Perfectionists zero in on mistakes. Challenge yourself to find at least three positives in every activity. Look for and find the extraordinary in the everyday. It's always there, you just need to focus the lens you are looking through in order to see it.

- **Take baby steps:** Perfectionists tend to set lofty, hard to reach goals that leave little room for error. They get discouraged when they fall short even though there might have been plenty of positives along the way. If you set smaller attainable goals and reward successes at various stages on the journey, you will tend to be more forgiving of mistakes. This is a more incremental approach and therefore takes longer, but in fact it can generate more satisfying and lasting successes.

Striving to always give your best effort is a commendable quality. The pursuit of excellence is a worthwhile pursuit – it is about striving for your personal best, not perfection. Excellence focuses on the process of achievement rather than the outcome. The pursuit of excellence welcomes help but perfectionism pushes it away. Do not let "perfect" be the enemy of "good."

I consider asking for help to be a skill. If it's something that you are not comfortable doing, then you should make getting better at it a personal goal. It is an important skill to learn. What are some of the benefits of asking for help? Psychologist Coert Visser has identified five specific benefits:[2]

1. **Better and faster progress:** When you ask for help, other people bring their experience and expertise to the problem and they can help move you forward.

2. **Reinforcement of a growth mindset in yourself:** People with a fixed mindset often see asking for help as sign of inability while people with a growth mindset often see it as a sensible step forward.

3. **Increase in relatedness:** Relatedness refers to the social nature of human beings and connectedness with others. Most humans have a natural psychological need to have meaningful and caring relationships with

other people. Asking for help gives you an opportunity to receive attention and help from another person and it thereby satisfies your need for relatedness.

4. **Opportunity to be grateful:** When we receive help, we are naturally grateful. Feeling grateful has several positive effects such as the production of serotonin and dopamine in the brain, improvement of sleep, reduction of stress and physical complaints, and the reduction of fear and depression.

5. **The helper feels good:** When you ask for help, you give the person helping an opportunity to share their talents and helping others feels good.

Successful people often say that the key to success is knowing your own strengths and weaknesses. They say to play to your strengths, surround yourself with people who are strong in areas you are not, and ask for help when you need it. Successful people get things done and they see asking for help as just part of the overall process.

But to many people, asking for help can be hard.

Why?

It's because asking for help can often be connected with feelings of fear, judgement and failure. Don't be held back by your pride or discomfort. Focus on the upside. Easier said than done, right? It definitely takes practice, but it is a learnable skill. Like anything, the more you do it the easier it gets. The reality is that much of the anxiety around asking for help is in our own head.

Most people overwhelmingly choose to be generous to others. People want to help but you have to ask.

Here are a few points that can be useful when asking for help:

- **Don't leave it until it's too late:** The sooner you open up about a problem the easier it will be to solve.

- **Demonstrate that you have tried to help yourself:** People are more inclined to help others when they see an honest effort has been made to solve the problem independently.

- **Be clear about what you need help with:** When you are clear about the problem, others can quickly determine if their experience and skill set are a match to resolving the problem.

- **Choose carefully who you ask for help:** Ask for help from those you trust or those who can be trusted. If you have a basis of trust with someone or due to their position they are bound by professional duty and a code of ethics, they are much less likely to take advantage of your vulnerability.

- **Find your tribe:** It is often easier to ask for help from people who closely relate to your situation or have been in your shoes.

- **Give a heart-felt thank you:** It is not just basic politeness but it's part of an important feedback loop to the one who helped. If their actions made a positive difference, let them know.

- **Pass it on:** Use your experience and talents to help others.

There is wisdom in the saying "If you want to go fast, go alone; but if you want to go far, go together." For some of the challenges we face in life, it is helpful and comforting to be part of a team. Help comes from fellow team members who bring their individual talents and skills to the group. When an effective team comes together, the whole really is greater than the sum of the parts. There is great positive energy, an *esprit de corps*, when people in a group share a common enthusiasm and work together toward a common goal. With multiple people involved in implementation of the plan and in outlining the vision and strategies, the footprint of effective impact is more widely useful. High-performance teams are made up of individuals who encourage and support their colleagues. Different talents will be called upon at different times and when one member falters there is another to help carry the load. According to the TESI[3] (Team Emotional and Social Intelligence) model, there are seven key elements to an effective team:

1. **Team identity:** A group with a strong team identity has a high degree of loyalty. Members feel that they belong and are valued and want to contribute to the success of the team.

2. **Motivation:** A motivated team has high energy and individuals perform to the best of their ability and are eager to take on new responsibilities.

3. **Emotional awareness:** When team members pay attention to, understand and respect the feelings of their colleagues, the group is able to function at a high level and be successful.

4. **Communication:** Communication is essential to a team achieving a common goal. Poor communication leads to splintering within the group and a lack of cohesive effort.

5. **Stress tolerance:** A team with good stress tolerance can roll with the punches. Team members come together to find a way through difficult times, and they support each other when times get tough.

6. **Conflict resolution:** An effective team does not get caught up in conflict. The group deals with adversity and individuals do not let disagreements break up the team and divert energy from achieving the group goals.

7. **Positive mood:** This is a major factor in a team's flexibility and resilience, and it is the heart of a "can-do" attitude.

Seek out opportunities in life to be part of a team. Teams are complex systems and when you engage in that environment you have the opportunity to learn a great deal about yourself. You get the chance to find out how others see you. Both your best and worst qualities will be highlighted. You can showcase only your best self when operating alone but there is no hiding the complete "you" in a team.

When the going gets tough, the tough ask for help. Don't see asking for help as a weakness but as a skill and an opportunity for growth. When you view asking for help in this way, you will see that it is right in line with the ABC... Always Be Correcting philosophy of life.

When you need help, ask for it.

You'll be happy that you did.

In Flight Checks

- When was the last time you asked for help?

- Do you resist asking for help and if so why?

- What is it like for you to admit to another that you need help?

CHAPTER EIGHT

NEW HORIZONS

*"I am not the same having seen the moon
shine on the other side of the world"*

MARY ANNE RADMACHER

Richard Branson, British entrepreneur, adventurer and head of the Virgin Group Ltd., once said, "Every success story is a tale of constant adaptation, revision and change."

There's great energy and wisdom in that statement. First of all, it emphasizes that a critical element of success is work. Constant work. Hard work. Work with a desire for improvement. Much of that hard work needs to be on adapting to change and correcting to the ideal.

To maximize the benefits of the ABC process, we should be correcting consistently, not just occasionally.

Life is always changing around us. Change really is the only constant in life. The good times don't last forever and neither do the bad. When you accept this, then you start to appreciate all the little moments in your life, knowing that you must enjoy them while you can. Constant change means that everything is temporary.

Second, there's a critical response element to success. It is a response element and not a reaction element. A reaction happens in an instant. It is based in the moment and is survival oriented. When we react, the subconscious mind is running the show. That means that we are not taking the long-term effects of our actions into consideration. We might get lucky and things turn out fine in the end or we might regret our actions in the long term. A response, on the other hand, is a slower process. It is based on information from both the conscious and subconscious mind. A response considers alternative actions, the effects of our actions on others and whether our actions are in line with our core values. So, in order to achieve success, we must always be correcting but it's not a knee-jerk correction. It is a more thoughtful correction.

Hopefully, through the process of adapting, revising and changing, we grow, and our horizon is broadened. At any point in time, our horizon is made up of our thoughts, ideas, opinions, values, experiences and perspectives. If we are to broaden our horizon, we must expose ourselves, through new experiences, to other thoughts, ideas, opinions, values and perspectives.

Most successful people that I admire place a great deal of importance on personal growth and development. They are focused on constantly learning and improving. If we have a goal of continuous personal development, then we must get out of our personal comfort zones.

One way to do that is to seek out opposites. We will like some of the ideas, opinions, values, and perspectives and we can adopt or blend them with those we already have. Others will not be a good fit. What works for one person may not work for another. However, the process is always productive if our takeaway is an appreciation of another way of seeing the world and a better understanding that there are a variety of ways of living a meaningful life.

Travel is an excellent way to seek out opposites. When we leave the comforts of home, we become hyper aware of what is different. Travel can expose us to new smells, foods, customs, weather, languages, rules, technology, religions, politics and so much more. Travel is a crash course in expanding our horizons.

When I travelled to Haiti on a United Nations tour with the Canadian Armed Forces in 1996, I was exposed to a level of poverty, political structure, traditions and customs I had never experienced before. Even communication was difficult. I am able to speak some French but in Haiti many of the people only speak Haitian Creole. It is a French-derived language, but the grammar is very different. The Haitian children in the villages had a fun time teaching me how to speak their language. I carried around a notepad in which I wrote down any new Creole words which I learned from the locals. Through fragmented communication conducted by references to my notepad, I learned about the joys and struggles of the Haitian people.

Experiences like that leave an impact.

However, one does not have to travel to one of the poorest countries in the western hemisphere for travel to have a dramatic impact. You just have to be open to new ideas and to living in the moment when you encounter what is new and different.

Over the past 30 years, the number of U.S. citizens holding a passport has increased dramatically. It presently stands at roughly 42% of the population. However, the share of passport holders in the United States still lags far behind other developed countries. The number is 66% in Canada, while in the UK, 76% of the people in England and Wales have a passport.[1]

Travel that requires a passport can be quite expensive. Not everyone can afford the cost or the time away from their work to travel to foreign countries. However, if you approach travel as an adventure in search of new, then the benefits of travel are not restricted to those who board a plane and bring back experiences from the other side of the world.

You often don't have to go very far to see a different way of life and learn something new. Traditions are sometimes practiced only in single cities or towns. Customs can be unique to parts of a country. Get out and explore the places near where you live. Meet people who have a different history and celebrate life in ways different from your own. Approach "different" with an open mind. You might be surprised by what you take away from the experience.

The multi-talented Danny Kaye once said, "To travel is to take a journey into yourself." When we travel, what we know and take as standard is challenged. That is not a bad thing. In fact, it should be embraced because that is how we learn and grow. There is no one way to live a happy life. When we travel, we increase our understanding of the world and the common issues of life.

Connecting with people who think very differently from the way we think is a great way to broaden our horizons.

Engaging in discussion with people who hold different, or even opposite political, religious and social views is not something we should shy away from. In fact, it is something we should seek out, in a careful way, if we hope to learn and grow. It is so easy for us to live in our own bubble.

Life is easy that way, isn't it?

It's safe—we have nobody challenging and nobody pointing out flaws in our logic. We have nobody asking us to explain our way of thinking or approach to life. Life inside our bubble can be a life where we are always right but limited by our experiences. Surrounding ourselves with people who think just like us is not the best way to grow and change. In fact, it can be a problem. It can lead to cognitive bias encouraging us to make inferences about others and situations from our subjective reality, while believing our opinions are the absolute truth. The more diverse your social and work groups, the more opportunities you have to learn and grow.

Engaging with different cultures can inspire you to learn new languages, explore new traditions, and gain valuable insights. Diversity helps you see a wider range of choices. Some of the choices you may find interesting and decide to explore. Others you may find just don't line up with your personality or even your values. If you approach the experience with an open mind, connecting with people who have different backgrounds is always valuable because it helps you see things from a different perspective.

It is narrow minded and quite arrogant to think that your way of life is the only way to be happy or the only reasonable option. This blue marble flying through space that we all call home is filled with people who all have the right to be different. There is no one way to live. People have different histories, different traditions and different beliefs. There are many benefits in getting to know people who are different from you.

Different opens you up to new experiences.

Different may arouse your curiosity.

Different might widen your perspective.

The next time that you run into someone with different ideas, traditions or beliefs than you, don't immediately try and convince them how you are right, and they are wrong. Instead, be curious. Ask them questions. Get to know them as individuals. Hear their experiences without judging them.

Burst your bubble.

Break down the walls of your echo chamber.

Discussions about politics, religion, history, and social issues often get to the core of someone's identity. It could be argued that if we avoid having such conversations then we really don't truly know each other. At the very least you can walk away from the experience having made a human connection, hopefully having learned something new and ideally having increased your empathy for other people.

Here are a few ideas to think about when it comes to conversations with people who have very different viewpoints than yours:[2]

- **Decide if you want to go there:** Ask yourself why you are thinking of having the conversation in the first place? Do you genuinely want to learn about someone's traditions and beliefs or are you looking to change their mind? The first reason can lead to interesting conversation with learning on both sides. If you start out with the intention of changing someone's mind, then that is not a conversation; it's a lecture.

- **Ask if you can ask about it:** It is important to appreciate that just because you might want to talk about a challenging topic doesn't mean the other person wants to as well. It's basic curtesy to ask if the subject is fair game for discussion and it's important to give the other person an out so they don't feel pressured to engage.

- **Find areas where you agree:** The goal of productive conversations is to build understanding and learning for all parties. Actively listen to the other person about what is important to them and pick up on areas where you agree.

- **Keep it neutral:** Avoid polarizing language and personal attacks. Be mindful of your words and tone in the conversation.

- **Share speaking time:** A dialogue is a back and forth interaction with another person. If you monopolize all the speaking time you are not engaging in dialogue – you are ranting.

- **Share stories:** People are wired for storytelling. Stories make us experience information, as opposed to just consuming it. Share your stories and listen to theirs.

- **Know when to end the conversation:** In productive conversations, there are no winners or losers. After active listening and the exchange of personal stories, the end result may be that both parties simply disagree, and the conversation needs to end because there's nothing more to be gained by going round and round. That's perfectly OK. Sometimes, when lots of new information is brought to light, it is important to end a conversation with the understanding that it will continue in the future simply because there needs to be time for reflection.

Mixing things up can produce interesting results. In ecology, there is a concept called the "edge effect," which describes the extraordinary explosion of biodiversity that occurs when two or more separate eco-systems overlap. Land and water or forest and grassland would be common examples of natural overlapping eco-system. In the area of overlap, species from each eco-system can be found as well as unique species only found in the overlap zone due to the unique conditions.

Can the edge effect apply to our own experiences with other cultures and our ability to relate to each other and peacefully coexist on this planet? Interesting work has been done in how the edge effect can impact our creativity.

American social psychologist Adam Galinsky has found that people who have deep relationships with someone from another country become more creative and score higher on routine creativity tests. In one study, Mr. Galinsky looked at fashion collections presented by the world's top fashion houses over 21 seasons. He found that the foreign experiences of the creative directors predicted the creativity ratings of their collections. Exposure to other cultures and the formation of collaborative relationships with people who might have different values, beliefs, language and customs resulted in more creative fashion.[3]

When information keeps coming from the same place, we can find ourselves in a creativity echo chamber. Creativity and progress require fresh lines of thinking.

Research has found that the edge effect also impacts science. Harvard economics Professor Richard Freeman has found that published scientific research receives greater attention if the authors are ethnically diverse. Scientists who have a wide network of collaborators produce more ground-breaking science. Freeman found that papers written by people with different backgrounds were cited more often than those written by people all from the same group. Better science comes from collaborations between people from different laboratories, from different areas of the same country, and between countries. Diversity within a group has a positive impact on the ideas generated by the group.[4]

The magic really does happen outside our comfort zones. It always has and it always will. Stepping outside your comfort zone is not easy and is in no way a guarantee of success but it's where the "new" resides, and where the learning and the growth happens.

So stretch!

Burst your bubble. Seek out new ideas and listen to other opinions. Make connections on a human level.

When you educate yourself about different ways of living, you can see the world from different perspectives and through it all broaden your horizons.

It's a big beautiful world and life is short. Don't spend your days living in a bubble.

In Flight Checks

- What action can you take to broaden your perspective on life?

- How can you learn more about the needs, history, traditions, beliefs and values of the cultural groups in your community? How can you increase your engagement with those cultural groups?

- How can you overcome any hesitancy you may have to explore new horizons?

CHAPTER 9

AIR SUPPORT

"As you grow older, you will discover that you have two hands, one for helping yourself, the other for helping others."

SAM LEVENSON

We have looked at the importance of investing in ourselves. Now let's look at the importance of investing our time, talents and money in the service of others. Helping others is one of the secrets to a life that is happier, healthier and more meaningful.

As Mahatma Ghandi said, "The best way to find yourself is to lose yourself in the service of others."

The human brain may be hard-wired for altruism because helping others is good for the group. Helping others seems to result in helping everybody involved. Studies have shown that helping others boosts our happiness, increases life satisfaction, provides a sense of meaning, increases feelings of competence, improves our mood and reduces our stress.

Helping others feels good. It is also contagious.

When one person performs a good deed, it causes a chain reaction of altruistic acts which benefits the community. Humans are social beings and we want to be connected and feel close to others in our group.

If you are looking for some ideas on how to share your time and talents with others, here are a few suggestions:

BECOME A MENTOR

Mentorship is a relationship where someone with experience in a specific area helps guide a less experienced or less knowledgeable person so that they can reach their full potential. What skills do you possess which might be of service to someone who is looking to develop their competencies? How can you pass on your passion in a certain area to help someone discover potential in themselves?

Have you had a great mentor in your life?

Maybe you had a great teacher who not only fuelled your interest in a subject but inspired you to a lifelong journey of learning. Perhaps you had a great coach who not only changed your game but, in the process, changed your life. Or maybe you had a colleague at work who took you under their wing when you started and showed you how to do things more efficiently and effectively which enabled you to achieve greater job satisfaction.

If you have, think for a minute about the impact that person has had on you. They supported your growth and helped build your confidence. They made you a better life pilot. They helped you have a smoother flight. A great mentor is like an extra set of eyes in the cockpit of life. While you are focused on the airspeed indicator, they point out that you are losing altitude.

A great mentor teaches you to see the bigger picture.

Mentors do not need to be experts in the area in which they

are helping to guide the less experienced. They just need to be a little farther down the road that the less experienced person is traveling. Mentors need to have an understanding and empathy for what it feels like to be less experienced and they must have an eagerness to invest in the mentee's growth. Mentors need the ability and availability to commit real time and energy to mentoring.

These relationships are valuable at all ages but when mentors invest in the growth of young people, they can shape lives by helping to develop good habits and build self-confidence. According to the National Mentoring Partnership, 1 in 3 young people will grow up without a mentor.[1] If you choose to donate your time, energy, experience and expertise as a mentor with an organized program, you can have a huge influence on the life of a young person.

You might choose to be a mentor in the workplace. Work mentors can have a major impact on the job satisfaction of new team members when they invest time and pass on cultural knowledge in highlighting ways the work can be done more efficiently and more effectively.

Whatever mentor opportunity you choose, you will be rewarded for your efforts by seeing that you are making a real difference in someone's life.

VOLUNTEER

Time is our most valuable commodity. With each day that goes by we don't get more of it, we get less and less. However, we all get the same 24 hours each day so it's a case of setting priorities rather than not having the time. When we give of our time in the service of others, we give a valuable gift. We also get so much in return. The return benefit is often not fully appreciated until we immerse ourselves in the volunteering experience.

Ask a volunteer why they do it and you'll often get a passionate answer about the community relationships created, the joy in seeing one's efforts make a direct difference in the lives of others and the mental and physical health benefits of volunteering.

The 2018 Volunteering in America report found that 77.34 million adults (30.3 percent) volunteered through an organization in 2017. Altogether, Americans volunteered nearly 6.9 billion hours, worth an estimated $167 billion in economic value.[2]

The value of volunteering is being appreciated beyond economic impact. Post-secondary educational institutions are asking applicants about their volunteering experiences and employers are noticing and valuing volunteering work on resumes because they appreciate that volunteering shows a personal commitment to making an impact in the world.

DONATE BLOOD

Give blood and you can save a life. If you are looking for something you can do with your time in the service of others, then giving blood is a very simple act with huge impact. According to the American Red Cross, one donation can potentially save up to three lives and every 2 seconds someone in the US needs blood. Roughly 38% of the population is eligible to give blood and each year yet only 10% of those who are eligible actually do so.[3]

You don't have to wait for an event in your community. Why not organize a blood drive yourself? Contact your local blood services group and they will be happy to provide you with all the information. Basically, what you need to host a blood drive is a large open room with enough space to ensure donor privacy, volunteers who will help with recruiting, scheduling and event support, and of course you need donors. The blood services group will have all the recruitment tools, equipment, supplies and trained staff required to help you organize a successful blood drive.

RANDOM ACTS OF KINDNESS

Aesop's fable, The Lion & the Mouse, teaches us that no act of kindness, no matter how small, is ever wasted. The story goes that a lion was fast asleep when a timid mouse unexpectedly came upon the lion and in her fright and haste to get away, she ran across the lion's nose. This woke the lion who was not too pleased. The lion laid his huge paw angrily on the tiny creature with the intent to kill her. The mouse begged to be spared and said that if the lion spared her, she would one day repay the favour. The lion was much amused that the small mouse could ever help him, but he was generous and decided to let the mouse go. Some days later, while hunting his prey, the lion got entangled in a hunter's net. Unable to free himself, the lion let out an angry roar. The mouse recognized the roar and quickly found the lion struggling in the net. Running to one of the great ropes, the mouse gnawed it until it fell apart and soon the lion was free. The mouse then said, "You laughed when I said I would repay you. Now you see that even a mouse can help a lion."

No act of kindness, no matter how small is ever wasted. Bring a smile to somebody's face, make their day or possibly change their life with a random act of kindness. The ABC approach focuses us on the idea that the little things matter. What might be a little thing to you might be a big deal to someone else.

When we help others, we increase our empathy as we put the well-being of others at the forefront of our thinking. If we are to truly help someone, we must sense what they are feeling, see the world from their perspective and walk a mile in their shoes. When there is an empathetic connection, people feel understood, seen and appreciated. Empathy enhances our communities.

Lose yourself in the service of others and you might be amazed by what you find.

Kindness – pass it on.

In Flight Checks

- What skills do you possess which could be put in the service of others?

- What new ideas would you be willing to explore?

- What first step can you take in committing yourself to action?

CHAPTER 10

IT'S ALWAYS SUNNY ABOVE THE CLOUDS

*"Happiness is not something ready made.
It comes from your own actions."*

DALAI LAMA

Even on the stormiest and darkest of days, if you fly high enough and break through the clouds, you will be greeted by beautiful light and incredible views. Flying taught me that no matter what the weather is on the ground, it's always sunny above the clouds.

The lesson is one of hope. And as Andy Dufresne notably writes in *The Shawshank Redemption*, "Hope is a good thing, maybe the best of things…"

Whatever your present circumstances, believe that there is always the potential to get to a brighter place. The key is to work at it and to never give up trying. Every day, every job, every relationship is filled with opportunities to learn—if you apply the ABC process, you can limit your mistakes and catch problems when they are small.

When we ask ourselves the two key questions that are at the core of the ABC process—"Where am I now?" and "Where do I want to go?"—we become active participants in our own lives.

We engage with life. These questions help us chart our own course. They give us a plan—a flight plan for life. Our engagement breathes life into the dreams, hopes and aspirations that are within each of us.

None of us know how many hours we will have in our logbook of life. The challenge as we fly through life is to live consciously and to appreciate that each moment is a gift. All you have is now.

Time is precious, and if you don't focus on the present and live in the moment, you might wake up one day and wonder where all the time went.

Focus on just *being*.

When you pay attention you notice the minor problems which, if left uncorrected, can lead to much bigger problems down the road. Being mindful will bring into focus the little wonders of life that reveal the extraordinary in the everyday.

In the end, the little things are in fact the big things in life.

It is important not to get down on yourself if you have a list of things you want to correct in your life. Grab a jersey and welcome to the team. We all have a list. Don't be upset if you recognize that you have failed to notice problems, or have chosen to ignore small issues in the hope that they would magically go away. My hope is that the message you take away from the ABC process is a positive one. The past is the past. You can't relive the past, but you can learn from it.

If you are fully committed to actioning change and to making it stick, then push that throttle forward and soon you will be breaking through the clouds to sunny skies. You are the pilot of your flight through life. The controls are in your hands. Remember ABC…Always Be Correcting.

Safe flying my friend and when your wheels finally touch down and you are taxiing off the runway, may you look back over your flight and say with a smile on your face, "Wow… what a wonderful adventure!"

REFERENCES

CHAPTER TWO

1. Inc., P. (n.d.). The Global Leader in Change Management Solutions. Retrieved from https://www.prosci.com/

2. Duhigg, C. (2014). *The Power of Habit Why We Do What We Do in Life and Business.* New York: Random House.

CHAPTER THREE

1. Ethical Principles of Psychologists and Code of Conduct. (n.d.). Retrieved September 24, 2020, from https://www.apa.org/ethics/code

2. 7 Great Reasons Why Exercise Matters. (2019, May 11). Retrieved from https://www.mayoclinic.org/healthy-lifestyle/fitness/in-depth/exercise/art-20048389

3. Manson, J. E., Greenland, P., Lacroix, A. Z., Stefanick, M. L., Mouton, C. P., Oberman, A., …Siscovick, D. S. (2002). Walking Compared with Vigorous Exercise for the Prevention of Cardiovascular Events in Women. *New England Journal of Medicine, 347(10), 716-725.* doi:10.1056/nejmoa021067

4. Brown, B. (2020, May 04). 14 Ways Reading Improves Your Mind and Body (Infographic). Retrieved from https://experteditor.com.au/blog/brain-books-benefits-reading/

5. Fagan, A. (2018, May 02). 6 Scientific Reasons You Should Be Reading More. Retrieved from https://www.mentalfloss.com/article/541158/scientific-reasons-you-should-read-more

6. Bavishi, A., Slade, M. D., & Levy, B. R. (2016). A Chapter a Day: Association of Book Reading with Longevity. *Social Science & Medicine, 164, 44-48.* doi:10.1016/j.socscimed.2016.07.014

7. Use of Yoga and Meditation Becoming More Popular in U.S. (2018, November 08). Retrieved from https://www.cdc.gov/nchs/pressroom/nchs_press_releases/2018/201811_Yoga_Meditation.htm

8. Gates, B. (2018, December 3). Why I'm Into Meditation. Retrieved from https://www.gatesnotes.com/Books/The-Headspace-Guide-to-Meditation-and-Mindfulness

9. The Tim Ferriss Show #444 [Audio blog interview]. (2020, June 26). Retrieved from https://tim.blog/2020/06/26/hugh-jackman/

10. 1 in 3 Adults Don't Get Enough Sleep. (2016, February 16). Retrieved from https://www.cdc.gov/media/releases/2016/p0215-enough-sleep.html

CHAPTER FOUR

1. Cancer Statistics. (2018, April 27). Retrieved from https://www.cancer.gov/about-cancer/understanding/statistics

2. Why is Early Diagnosis Important? (2019, March 04). Retrieved from https://www.cancerresearchuk.org/about-cancer/cancer-symptoms/why-is-early-diagnosis-important

3. Your Guide to Health Screenings by Age [INFOGRAPHIC]: Tri-City Medical Center. (2018, December 29). Retrieved from https://www.tricitymed.org/2016/09/guide-health-screenings-age-infographic/

4. Bouchez, C. (2009, July 20). Top 10 Ways to Boost Your Energy. Retrieved from https://www.webmd.com/women/features/10-energy-boosters#1

5. Rosekind, M. R., Smith, R. M., Miller, D. L., Co, E. L., Gregory, K. B., Webbon, L. L., …Lebacqz, J. V. (1995). Alertness Management: Strategic Naps in Operational Settings. *Journal of Sleep Research, 4, 62-66*. doi:10.1111/j.1365-2869.1995.tb00229.x

6. Flora, C. (2007, May 01). Gut Almighty. Retrieved from https://www.psychologytoday.com/ca/articles/200705/gut-almighty

7. Zulz, E. (2018, November 16). Daniel Kahneman: Your Intuition Is Wrong, Unless These 3 Conditions Are Met. Retrieved from https://www.thinkadvisor.com/2018/11/16/daniel-kahneman-do-not-trust-your-intuition-even-f/

8. Americans Spend Nearly Half of Their Waking Hours (42 percent) Looking at a Screen, It's Been Revealed by New Research. (2018, August 13). Retrieved from https://coopervision.com/our-company/news-center/press-release/americans-spend-nearly-half-their-waking-hours-42-percent

9. DiGiulio, S. (2017, May 30). Your Smartphone Is Changing the Human Race in Surprising Ways. Retrieved from https://www.nbcnews.com/storyline/the-big-questions/your-smartphone-may-actually-be-changing-human-race-n743866

CHAPTER FIVE

1. Ross, J., MD. (2020, June 17). Only the Overworked Die Young. Retrieved from https://www.health.harvard.edu/blog/only-the-overworked-die-young-201512148815

2. Grensing-Pophal, L. (2018, April 12). 4 Distinct Types of Corporate Culture-Which Is Yours? Retrieved from https://hrdailyadvisor.blr.com/2018/04/12/4-distinct-types-corporate-culture/

CHAPTER SIX

1. Stress in America: Paying with Our Health (Rep.). (2015, February 4). Retrieved from https://www.apa.org/news/press/releases/stress/2014/stress-report.pdf

2. Federal Reserve. (2017). *Changes in U.S. Family Finances from 2013 to 2016: Evidence from the Survey of Consumer Finances (Vol 103, No. 3)*. Retrieved from https://www.federalreserve.gov/publications/files/scf17.pdf

3. Marte, J. (2020, February 11). U.S. Household Debt Tops $14 Trillion and Reaches New Record. Retrieved from https://www.reuters.com/article/us-usa-fed-household-debt/u-s-household-debt-tops-14-trillion-and-reaches-new-record-idUSKBN20521Z

4. Debt to Income Ratio Calculator Canada. (n.d.). Retrieved from https://www.debt.ca/calculators/debt-to-income-ratio-calculator

5. Federal Trade Commission. (2012). *Report to Congress Under Section 319 of the Fair and Accurate Credit Transactions Act of 2003*. Retrieved from https://www.ftc.gov/sites/default/files/documents/reports/section-319-fair-and-accurate-credit-transactions-act-2003-fifth-interim-federal-trade-commission/130211factareport.pdf

6. Jacobe, D. (2020, January 06). One in Three Americans Prepare a Detailed Household Budget. Retrieved from https://news.gallup.com/poll/162872/one-three-americans-prepare-detailed-household-budget.aspx

CHAPTER SEVEN

1. Perfectionism. (2020). In *Merriam-Webster Dictionary*. Retrieved from https://www.merriam-webster.com/dictionary/perfectionism

2. Visser, C. (2015, May 25). 5 Benefits of Asking for Help [Web log post]. Retrieved from http://www.progressfocused.com/2015/05/5-benefits-of-asking-for-help.html

3. Lino, C. (2016). The Psychology of Teamwork: The 7 Habits of Highly Effective Teams. Retrieved from https://positivepsychology.com/psychology-teamwork/

CHAPTER EIGHT

1. McCarthy, N. (2018, January 11). The Share of Americans Holding A Passport Has Increased Dramatically in Recent Years [Infographic]. Retrieved from https://www.forbes.com/sites/niallmccarthy/2018/01/11/the-share-of-americans-holding-a-passport-has-increased-dramatically-in-recent-years-infographic/#2b07eec03c16

2. DiGiulio, S. (2019, September 30). 9 Tips for Talking to People You Disagree With. Retrieved from https://www.nbcnews.com/better/lifestyle/9-tips-talking-people-you-disagree-ncna1059326

3. Vedantam, S. (host). (2018, July 2). The Edge Effect [Audio podcast]. In Hidden Brain. Retrieved from https://www.npr.org/2018/07/02/625426015/the-edge-effect

4. Freeman, R., Huang, W. (2015, July). Collaborating with People Like Me: Ethnic Co-Authorship within the U.S. Journal of Labor Economics, Special Issue on High Skill Immigration. 2015;33 (3) :S289-S318. doi:10.1086/678973

CHAPTER NINE

1. Mentoring Impact. Connect with a Young Person. (n.d.). Retrieved from https://www.mentoring.org/mentoring-impact/

2. Volunteering in U.S. Hits Record High; Worth $167 Billion. (2018, November 13). Retrieved from https://www.nationalservice.gov/newsroom/press-releases/2018/volunteering-us-hits-record-high-worth-167-billion

3. Blood Needs & Blood Supply. (n.d.). Retrieved from https://www.redcrossblood.org/donate-blood/how-to-donate/how-blood-donations-help/blood-needs-blood-supply.html

ACKNOWLEDGEMENTS

I am grateful to many people for their contributions to this book.

I must start by thanking my ever-patient wife, Tara, who sat beside me on the roller coaster that is the writing experience. Thanks for sharing my excitement during the thrilling parts and holding my hand for the scary bits. I love you.

To my Mom & Dad, thank you for giving me the foundation and the values this book is built upon.

To my hard-working editors, thank you for all your help in polishing my ideas. Your valuable feedback and suggestions pushed me to dig deeper and find the quality nuggets.

To Greg, Neil, Terry and Royce, thank you for turning up the heat on an idea that had been simmering in my mind for some time. Who knew where our conversations would lead?

ABOUT THE AUTHOR

Peter Carroll is a former Captain in the Canadian Armed Forces, where he flew helicopters with 408 Tactical Helicopter Squadron and participated in a United Nations peacekeeping mission in Haiti. The life lessons and resilience that he learned in the military were really put to the test in his next career progression as a stay-at-home dad to his two wonderful kids. Not one to rest on his laurels, he has also been a professional photographer, a banking specialist, a human resources advisor and a member of Canada's Department of Veterans Affairs. He began writing this book to share how the lessons he learned in flight training have positively affected his life. Pete has a Mechanical Engineering degree from McGill University and a Human Resource Management Diploma from the Northern Alberta Institute of Technology, and lives in Edmonton with his wife and children. Connect with Pete by visiting **www.PeterCarroll.ca** or drop him a line at **aflightplanforlife@gmail.com**

Manufactured by Amazon.ca
Bolton, ON